JESSE JAMES
and the First Missouri Train Robbery

Marker erected at the Gads Hill robbery site in 1962 by the Piedmont Lions Club.

JESSE JAMES

and the First Missouri Train Robbery

Ronald H. Beights

PELICAN PUBLISHING COMPANY
Gretna 2002

*The word "Pelican" and the depiction of a pelican are trademarks
of Pelican Publishing Company, Inc., and are registered
in the U.S. Patent and Trademark Office.*

Library of Congress Cataloging-in-Publication Data

Beights, Ronald H.
  Jesse James and the first Missouri train robbery /
Ronald H. Beights.
      p. cm.
  Includes bibliographical references and index.
  ISBN 1-58980-019-2 (pbk.)
    1. James, Jesse, 1847-1882. 2. Outlaws—West (U.S.)—
Biography. 3. Train robberies—Missouri—Gads Hill—
History—19th century. 4. Gads Hill (Mo.)—History—19th
century. 5. Frontier and pioneer life—West (U.S.) 6.
Frontier and pioneer life—Missouri. I. Title.

F594.J27 B45 2002
364.15'52—dc21
                                              2001059818

Printed in Canada

Published by Pelican Publishing Company, Inc.
1000 Burmaster Street, Gretna, Louisiana 70053

Dedicated in loving memory to my father
Hugh F. Beights
who worked more than thirty-seven years
for the Missouri Pacific Railroad

In all the history of medieval knight errantry and modern brigandage, there is nothing that equals the wild romance of the past few years' career of Arthur McCoy, Frank and Jesse James and the Younger boys. . . . Their fame has become national, aye, world-wide. . . . They have captured and pillaged whole railroad trains. . . . They have dashed into towns and cleaned out banking-houses in broad daylight. . . . Detectives, who have undertaken to ferret them out, have been slain. Sheriff's posses have been routed. The whole State authorities defied and spit upon by this half-dozen brilliant, bold, indefatigable rough-riders.

—*Lexington (Missouri) Weekly Caucasian,* September 5, 1874

Contents

Preface

In the summer of 1947 I was a boy traveling with the family on a northbound Missouri Pacific passenger train from Poplar Bluff, Missouri, to visit my grandmother in Kansas City. We were passing through the Ozark foothills less than an hour from home when our friendly conductor pointed out a place called Gads Hill, site of one of Jesse James' famous train robberies. Wide-eyed, I peered from the coach window as we rumbled past the all but extinct settlement.

"Better hold on to your pocketbooks, folks," the conductor jokingly warned. "Jesse James and the boys might still be lurking out there in the brush somewhere!"

Although I was only eight years old, I knew the trainman was kidding us. Old Jesse could not have been lurking in the brush at Gads Hill nor anyplace else. He was dead. A "dirty little coward" had shot him down some years ago in a Tyrone Power movie. I'd seen it myself. Content in that knowledge, I settled back and returned to doing whatever it is eight-year-olds do to tolerate the boredom of travel. We later changed trains in St. Louis and, I am happy to report, made it safely to Kansas City and Grandma's house without being molested by outlaws.

That first glimpse of Gads Hill, Missouri, fleeting though it was, made an impression on my young mind that lingered long after we returned home. The rail line that had carried the plundered train south after the robbery in 1874, and us back home to Poplar Bluff in 1947, passed within two miles of my house. Oftentimes after our trip, I would lie in bed at night listening to the distant roar of modern trains traveling down that same old track and imagine the one of long ago, its hapless passengers still shivering with excitement over their recent confrontation with robbers. In boyish fantasy I could see the fabled Jesse, his brother Frank, and the Younger brothers, their pockets bulging with train loot and the sheriff's posse nipping at their heels, as they escaped on horseback over the timbered hills of northwestern Wayne County. Entertained by those mental images of railroad trains, outlaws, and pursuing lawmen, I would drift quietly off to sleep.

In time the childhood fantasies passed, but my interest in Jesse James and Gads Hill did not. The fact that this famous badman of the Old West had robbed a train so near my home continued to intrigue me. During my teenage years, I listened intently as the old folks told wild stories about Frank and Jesse; of the boys generously sharing their ill-gotten wealth with poor families along the escape route; of local caves where they were supposed to have hid out or stashed loot; and of the gnarled old tree, then still standing at Gads Hill, where legend claimed Jesse tied his horse. How many of those tales were true, and how many were folklore, I had no idea.

Wishing to know the facts, I read numerous books on Jesse James, but they were somewhat confusing. While most presented interesting versions of the Gads Hill robbery, the details were usually very brief and varied widely from one account to the next. Several years ago, still hounded by a lingering curiosity, I began doing my own research on that historic raid, and unexpectedly an old boyhood enthusiasm was reborn. The more I learned, the more I wanted to know. Before long a casual interest had grown into a mild obsession, and at some point I decided to write my own Jesse James book—one focusing primarily on Gads Hill and events related to the crime.

In 1989 while visiting St. Joseph, Missouri, I had the great privilege to meet the well-known historian Milton Perry, then director and curator of Clay County Recreation and Historic Sites. Mr. Perry was a former curator at the U.S. Military Academy's West Point Museum and from 1958 to 1976 held the position of curator at the Harry S. Truman Library and Museum in Independence. He was also a leading authority on Jesse James. When I told Mr. Perry I was considering writing a book about the Gads Hill train robbery, he liked the idea. He said he had long believed there was ample material to warrant books on each of the James brothers' robberies and felt that "sprightly written" documented histories would not only be of interest to the general reader, but would serve as scholarly works for future researchers as well. Inspired, I returned home and began my study in earnest.

Determined to produce an honest and factual account, I turned to the most authentic sources available—recorded statements from passengers, trainmen, farmers, detectives, and others who had confronted the bandits before, during, or after the robbery. There was also much to be gleaned from contemporary news articles, period maps, old letters, county history books, field trips to locations the outlaws supposedly visited, and even stories handed down from local old-timers. Countless hours were spent poring over stacks of ancient materials, checking and cross-checking information, using both fact and logic to separate the reliable from the not-so-reliable. It was a monumental task, this research, but the rewards came. Slowly, from the mist of the past emerged details of an exciting Jesse James outlaw adventure as it had actually happened—without the glamor and romance of a Hollywood movie nor the embellishment of imaginative writers. Here, at the peak of their careers, were Jesse and his notorious gang on a month-and-a-half-long, 700-mile horseback romp across Arkansas and Missouri, robbing, running from the law, stopping to eat and sleep at farmhouses, and engaging in deadly confrontations with pursuing detectives.

It was a story that had never been fully told, and I was eager to tell it.

The train raid at Gads Hill proved to be a major turning point in the careers of the James and Younger brothers. Robin Hood-like incidents that occurred during the robbery, retreat, and pursuit not only brought these bandits worldwide attention but became a major source for much of the Jesse James legend we know today. To explore some of the facts behind that legend and, more importantly, to preserve as accurately as possible the historic details of Missouri's first train robbery, this book was written.

Acknowledgments

Researching and writing even this small bit of Jesse James history was no easy task, and I daresay that without the interest and generous help of a number of special individuals it could never have been accomplished.

First and foremost I wish to thank my dear sister Saralie Morgan, for neatly and professionally typing the manuscript and for so patiently making the multitudinous copy changes I dumped on her over a period of several months. She also assisted enormously in various phases of the research and from time to time offered suggestions that proved invaluable. Thanks, Saralie!

Another extremely important contributor to the completion of this work was my very good friend, former high-school English teacher Harris Maupin. Harry was kind enough to take time from his busy retirement to proofread the manuscript carefully and make a great number of much-needed corrections in sentence structure and punctuation.

Long before the writing, typing, and proofreading, however, came the research, and that research would have been utterly impossible without the numerous libraries and historical organizations that have been so helpful to me over the years. In particular I wish to thank the accommodating staffs at the St. Louis Public Library; the State Historical Society of

Missouri, Columbia; the Missouri Historical Society, St. Louis; the Arkansas History Commission, Little Rock; the Illinois Historical Society, Springfield; the Minnesota Historical Society, St. Paul; and the Carondelet Historical Society, St. Louis. I would especially like to thank (in spirit) the late Dale L. Walker, archivist of the Missouri Pacific Historical Society in St. Louis, for sending material and answering scads of questions regarding railroads and old-time trains.

I also owe a big debt of gratitude to the many who shared old stories, articles, family records, and photographs and to those who helped in other ways with information or material often unattainable from any other source. Listed here in alphabetical order—although not necessarily in order of importance—are most of those people. Hopefully, each knows his or her contributions and how grateful I am for the help received. With apologies for any omissions, the list includes: Velma Adams; Gilbert K. Alford, Jr.; Brick Autry; Virgil Clubb; Harry Diesel; Brian Driscoll; Tim Eaton; Fern George; Mike Holifield; Charlene Hopkins; Robert Howell; Norman Keele; Carl Laxton; Amel Martin; Coker Montgomery; Hamil Montgomery; J. L. Moss; Jack Myers; Kent Dean Nichols; Cheryl Oberhaus; Richard Owings; Jeanette Parker; Gary Parkin; my sister Carolyn Ponte; Marjorie Mason Robinson; Bill Royce; Bob Ruble; Bill Saenger; Marty Schuster; Leona Sutterfield Skelton; Angie Smith; Ray Smith; Floyd Sutterfield; Richard Thaler; J. J. Tinsley; Cameron E. Ward; Julie Warren; Alice Fitz White; Tom Williams; and Kati Wylie of the Butler County (Missouri) Historical Society.

Another group of individuals I truly appreciate are the Jesse James writers and historians who have preceded me. Although our interpretations of facts may sometimes differ slightly, their documented accounts have been for me an abundant source of information and inspiration. They all have my utmost admiration and respect. I specifically want to thank Marley Brant and Wilbur Zink for answering questions regarding the

Younger-Pinkerton gunfight and Phillip Steele for assisting me with book publishing information.

Also, I am much indebted to a friend of many, the late James historian, Milton F. Perry, who first encouraged me to write this book. For our chance meeting in St. Joseph, Missouri, in 1989, and for our correspondence afterward, I will always be grateful.

I, of course, want to say a very special thank you to Nina Kooij and the folks at Pelican Publishing Company for seeing potential in this true story of Jesse James and for giving me the opportunity to tell it.

To family and friends: Thank you for your continual support, encouragement, and prayers.

And finally, on a lighter note, it is probably fitting that I should give a tip of the hat to Frank and Jesse James for choosing to live outside the law. Obviously, had they not been so ornery, this book would never have been written.

The Missouri Outlaws

A great war leaves the country with three armies—an army of cripples, an army of mourners, and an army of thieves.
—German proverb

Of all the bank and train robbers in American history, Frank and Jesse James were without a doubt the most famous and successful. The tools of their trade were the horse and revolver, and they became masters of both while riding as mere boys in Confederate guerrilla bands during the Civil War. Under the tutelage of such notorious leaders as William Clarke Quantrill, "Bloody Bill" Anderson, and George Todd, these young farm lads from Clay County, Missouri, developed the reckless hit-and-run fighting tactics that would remain their trademark throughout the many years of civilian banditry that lay ahead.

When the South surrendered in 1865, Missouri's defeated ex-Confederates returned home to an uneasy peace. Wounds of bitterness wrought by the war were slow in healing, and readjustment to civilian life proved extremely difficult—for some more than others. To add to rebel woes, the Radical Republican Party, then in control of Missouri's provisional government, had adopted a new state constitution that weighed heavily against Missourians who had fought for the South. Under this new law the state's former rebels were forbidden to vote, seek public office, attend college, engage in principal professions, become ministers of the gospel, or even serve as church deacons. And while amnesty was provided to Union boys for any atrocities they might have committed during the war, Southern boys were still held accountable for such acts and subject to prosecution. This one-sided law would remain in effect for several years.

Most ex-Confederates in western Missouri, even those who had ridden under the "black flag" of Quantrill, Anderson, and Todd, were somehow able to turn the other cheek and settle down peaceably. Others refused. Within a year after their surrender many had returned to the saddle and were back at their old habits of raiding and pillaging. Now, however, it was done not in the name of the Confederacy, but solely for personal gain.

The first of these postwar raids occurred February 13, 1866, when a dozen or so of the old Quantrill bunch rode horseback and armed into Liberty, Missouri, and cleaned out the Clay County Savings Bank of more than sixty thousand dollars in currency and negotiable government bonds. That historic event, America's first daylight peacetime bank robbery, took place just fifteen miles from the James boys' home. It would be followed by a long series of spectacular bank, stagecoach, and train robberies charged to these outlaw brothers spanning a sixteen-year period and encompassing at least eight Midwestern and Southern states. Frank and Jesse James, Cole Younger and his brothers, and the many who rode with them would forever blame the Civil War for their troubles, claiming that mistreatment by Northern radicals had "driven" them into outlawry.

By 1873 the James-Younger gang, as they came to be called, were already the most hunted outlaws in America. Besides robbing Liberty, they were suspected of bank raids at Lexington, Missouri; Savannah, Missouri (a failed attempt); Richmond, Missouri; Russellville, Kentucky; Gallatin, Missouri; Corydon, Iowa; Columbia, Kentucky; and Ste. Genevieve, Missouri. Also on their list of crimes was the ticket-gate holdup at the Kansas City fair, during which a shot fired at the cashier missed and inflicted a painful flesh wound in the leg of a little girl.[1] In all, outlaw gunfire had injured eight citizens—five of them fatally.

The first peacetime train robbery charged to Jesse James— he would do six in all—took place July 21, 1873, about four miles west of Adair, Iowa. At dusk that day a band of men masked as Ku Klux Klansmen loosened a section of track on the Chicago, Rock Island and Pacific Railroad and hid in nearby brush. When the slow-moving train rounded the curve, they drew the rail out of line by pulling an attached rope. As expected, the train jumped the track and ground to a stop, but, tragically, the locomotive toppled onto its side killing the engineer. The bandits reportedly extracted about two thousand dollars from the express car and finished the job by collecting cash and valuables from the shaken passengers. A sheriff's posse trailed them southward into Missouri but came back empty-handed. The *St. Joseph Morning Herald* accused Jesse James of being the gang's leader.[2]

By that time, hired detectives were searching high and low for the brigands, and large rewards were being offered for their capture. Yet, through it all, Jesse and his followers continued to evade all pursuers and to raid and plunder almost at will. As they did, their legend grew.

While most citizens rightly viewed the Missouri outlaws as thieves and murderers, many actually saw them as bigger-than-life heroes of the Lost Cause, misunderstood and fighting against social injustice and persecution. Southern-minded journalists began comparing them to the knights of old England and their exploits to those of such celebrated outlaws as Dick Turpin, Claude Duval, or the fictitious Robin Hood, who robbed the rich and gave to the poor. Some, like *St. Louis Dispatch* editor John Newman Edwards—himself a former Confederate major and, not coincidentally, a close personal friend of the James brothers—even claimed that Jesse, Frank, and the Younger boys had, for the most part, been falsely accused and he wrote strongly in their defense.[3]

On December 29, 1873, a letter bearing Jesse James' signature appeared in the *Dispatch*. It insisted that Jesse and Frank were guiltless of all recent crimes, offered alibis for same, and stated they would be willing to surrender if the governor would only assure them a fair trial and protection against lynch mobs. Probably written with Edwards' help, the letter claimed that Jesse was then living in faraway Deer Lodge, Montana Territory, a story that was as unlikely as his innocence.

But wherever Jesse James might have been in late 1873, his whereabouts in early 1874 is all but certain. During the first two months of the new year, a number of horse and revolver robberies occurred in the middle Southern sections of the country, and the James brothers appear to have taken part in at least two of them. One was a stagecoach holdup near the popular resort town of Hot Springs, Arkansas. The other was the infamous train raid at Gads Hill, Missouri—the focus of our book.

The reader is invited to come along now on a long journey into America's past as we travel by stagecoach, train, and horseback over old roads and long-forgotten trails to the days when the James and Younger boys rode and pillaged the land. Our story begins not with the robbery at Gads Hill, but many miles to the south, in Arkansas, eighteen days earlier.

JESSE JAMES
and the First Missouri Train Robbery

PART I

The Journey to Gads Hill

Frank James at about twenty-one years of age. (Courtesy of the State Historical Society of Missouri, Columbia)

CHAPTER 1

A Bit of Mischief in Arkansas

The Feats of Dick Turpin Eclipsed—One of the Most Daring
Highway Robberies Ever Committed
—(Headline) *Little Rock Arkansas Gazette,* January 18, 1874

On the morning of Tuesday, January 13, 1874, five mysterious
horsemen, now believed to have been Frank and Jesse James,
two of the Younger brothers, and perhaps either Clell Miller or
Arthur McCoy, were seen riding out of Arkadelphia, Arkansas,
northeast along the Cairo and Fulton Railroad.[1] Witnesses
would later recall that each man was equipped with several
navy revolvers, one wore a cartridge belt, and three carried
breechloading double-barreled shotguns. All wore blue
Federal Army overcoats. Their horses were of fine thorough-
bred stock, sleek and built for speed. Behind their saddles
were bedrolls, extra clothing, maps, and other gear common
to overland travelers.

Although the strangers attracted some attention, the towns-
people were not overly concerned. After all, the men seemed
peaceable enough, and it was not unusual in those post-Civil
War days for travelers to go armed. The good people of
Arkadelphia watched them pass and then casually returned to
their various activities. Only later would they learn that five
days earlier, five similar men had robbed a stagecoach near

Arcadia, Louisiana, a hundred miles to the south, and fled north in their general direction. It would be speculated, though never proven, that these Arkansas travelers and the Louisiana stage robbers were one and the same group.[2]

That evening, the party reined up at the home of a Mr. Easley, who lived near the railroad line twelve miles southwest of Malvern. In those days, traveling men often stopped at rural houses along the way and paid for food and lodging. Farmers were usually happy to have the company and were always able to use the extra cash. When the men asked for those accommodations, Easley obliged. After a comfortable night's sleep and breakfast the next morning, they resumed their journey.

A few miles farther up the track, they turned their horses northwest into the Ouachita foothills and by nightfall were eating supper at the Price home about ten miles east of Hot Springs. After supper the menfolk retired to the parlor to smoke and talk. Mr. Price later said that his heavily armed guests told him they were trailing horse thieves and sometime during the evening's conversation asked about the old stage road from Benton.[3]

According to news reports, the men left Price's home at sunup and continued to ride west toward Hot Springs. They apparently spent a few hours in that resort town relaxing and taking in the sights, and it is believed that while there Jesse went to a photography studio and had his picture taken.[4] The men would not be heard from again until midafternoon, when they were seen crossing Gulpha Creek about five miles from Price's. They were then traveling back east in the direction of Malvern. It was Thursday, January 15. The state of Arkansas was about to be officially introduced to the outlaw Jesse James.

At noon that day a four-horse Concord coach of the El Paso Stage Company had set out from Malvern on its routine westerly run to Hot Springs, a distance of twenty-four miles. Accompanying the coach were two ambulances (light road wagons), the seats of which could be folded into beds to

This photograph of Jesse James is believed to have been taken at a studio in Hot Springs, Arkansas, just hours before he and his gang robbed the westbound stage. A witness to the robbery said "the chief of the gang wore a belt filled with cartridges." (Courtesy of Phillip W. Steele)

accommodate the "invalid" passengers. The window curtains were drawn to keep out the cold. On board were the drivers, eleven male passengers, an express box, and a few sacks of United States mail.

At shortly past 3:00 P.M. the stage and ambulances reached Gulpha Creek and the valley farm of a locally prominent family named Gaines. There beside the road, about five miles from Hot Springs, was a rest area where drivers regularly stopped to water their horses. Contemporary writer J. A. Dacus, who was obviously familiar with this bit of geography, described it as "a narrow dell, shut in by abrupt hills, clad with a dense forest of pine and tangled underbrush and evergreen vines." He continued, "At this particular place the valley widens, and there is a beautiful farm and lovely grounds bordering the roadside on the east and north side of the stream. West and south the deep, tangled forest crowns the hills, which rise to a great height."[5] The Gaines mansion stood about two hundred yards to the northeast. Because of its proximity, stage drivers commonly referred to this rest area simply as the "Gaines Place."

There the vehicles stopped. As the horses drank their fill and the passengers stretched and walked about, five armed riders passed coming from the direction of Hot Springs. They were well mounted, it was noticed, and all wore Federal Army overcoats of the late Civil War. The unsuspecting stage travelers paid little heed to these blue-coated strangers and were soon refreshed, back aboard, and off on the last leg of their journey to the Springs. Each man no doubt was eagerly looking forward to the comforts of a warm hotel room, a leisurely evening meal, and a soothing mineral bath at one of the town's numerous thermal spas.

The cavalcade had proceeded only about half a mile when the stage driver heard a rumble of horses' hooves approaching from the rear. Looking back, he saw the same five riders who had passed them at the creek—and they were coming now at full gallop with guns drawn! One man was masked, a witness later said; the others were only partially. As they overtook the stage, the lead rider leveled a double-barreled shotgun at the driver and reportedly shouted, "Stop, or I'll blow your head off!"

At the time it mattered not to the stage driver that this shotgun wielder who threatened his life might have been the notorious Missouri outlaw Jesse James—or Satan himself for that matter. Of greater concern to this master of whip and reins was the fact that a loaded shotgun, with hammers at full cock, was pointing squarely at his bewhiskered face. Leaning back on the reins, applying the brake, and shouting the most sincere "whoa" of his stage-driving career, the shaken driver brought the team, himself, and his whole entourage to a skidding halt.

And there they sat, unarmed, helpless as so many sheep before their shearers.

One of the stage passengers was George R. Crump, a tobacco representative from Memphis. When Mr. Crump heard the commotion outside and raised the window curtain to have a look-see, he was rudely greeted by a man pointing a cocked navy revolver. Using a few rough adjectives appropriate to the occasion, the gunman ordered Crump and his fellow passengers to step out quick. One gentleman, badly crippled with "rheumatism," was allowed to remain in the coach, but the others promptly obeyed. The *Little Rock Arkansas Gazette* gave this account from Mr. Crump's testimony:

> They got out, and, as they did so, were ordered to throw up their hands. Three men were in front of them with cocked pistols and another with a shotgun, while on the other side of the stage was still another—all pointing their weapons toward the passengers and the driver. After getting the passengers out, they made them form in a kind of circle so that all of them could be covered by the pistols and gun. The leader then "went through" each passenger, taking all the watches, jewelry and money that could conveniently be found, that were of special value. . . . While the main party was engaged in this work, another took out the best horse in the coach, saddled him, rode up and down the road about fifty yards two or three times, and remarked that "he would do."[6]

Cole Younger, as a young man. (Courtesy of the State Historical Society of Missouri, Columbia)

The stolen horse became at that moment a spare mount to be used by the robbers in their planned retreat back to Missouri.

The express box was next looted, adding another $435 to the plunder. Several mail bags were also torn open as the robbers searched for registered letters containing money.

When the heist was at last completed, the leader, apparently wishing to find out if he had any enemies in the crowd, began interviewing his captives. Each passenger was asked his name and occupation, and judged accordingly. Some were treated kindly; others were subjected to a bit of verbal abuse.

George Crump later said that the "captain" asked if there were any "Southern men" among them. The *Arkansas Gazette* told it this way:

This ad appeared in the Little Rock Arkansas
Gazette, *January 15, 1874, the day Jesse James and
his gang robbed the Hot Springs stage.*

Mr. Crump spoke up, as did one or two others, that they were southern men. They then asked if there were any who had served in the confederate army during the war. Mr. Crump answered that he did. They questioned him as to what command, and remarking that he looked like an honest fellow, one who was telling the truth, handed him back his watch and money, saying they did not want to rob confederate soldiers; that the northern men had driven them into outlawry and they intended to make them pay for it.

Next approached was William Taylor of Massachusetts. The leader asked where he was from, and Taylor, perhaps concluding that being a genuine Northern Yankee would not be in his best interest at the moment, chose to lie.

"St. Louis," he responded.

The outlaw eyed him suspiciously.

"Yes," he said, "and you are a newspaper reporter for the *St. Louis Democrat,* the vilest paper in the West. Go to Hot Springs and send the *Democrat* a telegram about this affair, and give them my compliments."[7]

The interviewer moved on, but the other robbers continued taunting Mr. Taylor. Referring to him as the "*St. Louis Democrat* man," they laughingly remarked "about the exact parts of his body they could put lead through." The one wielding the shotgun was quoted as saying, "I'll bet I can shoot his hat off, without touching a hair of his head." They all seemed to be jolly fellows, according to Mr. Crump, and enjoyed the fun very much.

The passengers, on the other hand, enjoyed the fun very little, and the one who probably enjoyed it least was John A. Burbank, former governor of Dakota Territory. This distinguished gentleman had been forced to fork over $840 cash, a diamond stick pin of some value, and a monogrammed gold watch. Also snatched was his satchel containing important papers. When Burbank asked if the papers might be returned, the leader again became suspicious. The *Arkansas Gazette* reported:

The "captain" squatted down on his knees, and commenced examining them. Turning round to his followers he said, "Boys, I believe he is a detective—shoot him!" and forthwith, he was covered with three pistols. "Stop," said the chief, looking further, "I guess it's all right," and handed the governor his papers.

As the stage robbers mounted to leave, an unidentified passenger from Syracuse, New York, asked if five dollars of his money might be returned so he could telegraph home. His humble request was denied. "If you have no friends nor money," the outlaw chief allegedly said, "you had better go and die—you will be little loss anyway."

And on that cheery note the robbers galloped away, leaving the passengers to count their losses—and their blessings. The *Arkansas Gazette* gave the losses as follows:

> From Ex-Gov. Burbank, of Dakota, they obtained $840 in money, a diamond pin and gold watch. A gentleman named Taylor, from Lowell, Mass., went up for $650 in money. A passenger from Syracuse, N. Y., gave up his last nickle, $160. Mr. Johnny Dietrich, our boot and shoe merchant, lost $5 in money and a fine gold watch. He had $50 besides this in the watch pocket of his pants that they did not find. Mr. Charley Moore, of the ice house, gave up $70 in money and his silver watch, but they returned the latter, stating they did not want any silver watches. A Mr. Peoples, who resides near Hot Springs, lost $20. Three countrymen lost about $15. The express package, containing about $435 was also taken.

Mr. Crump initially surrendered his watch and about forty-five dollars in money, but it was all returned because he had served in the Confederate Army. The crippled passenger, who was allowed to remain in the coach, was not robbed.

Assuming the pilfered cash amounts were listed correctly, the total take in this robbery, excluding watches, jewelry, and the stolen stage horse, would have amounted to roughly $2,200. (The Friday morning *Little Rock Republican* reported the total figure at $2,000.)

Within an hour after the holdup, the stagecoach and its accompanying road wagons pulled up to the Sumpter Hotel in Hot Springs, and the Rice County sheriff was notified. He immediately organized a posse, but, due to the early darkness of winter, a meaningful search did not get under way until morning. By then the robbers were miles away.

And who were the robbers? No one knew yet, of course, but a reporter for the *Arkansas Gazette* had a pretty fair idea. He wrote, "From the talk of the 'Captain,' it is thought they were from Missouri. They took breakfast on the road between Malvern and Hot Springs . . . and, from the description, it is thought the chief is a celebrated Missouri brigand (whose name we now forget), who has been outlawed by the authorities of that state, and for whom there is a standing reward of $10,000."[8]

Reward or not, the "celebrated Missouri brigand" and his band of thieves were on their way back to the old home state— and a place called Gads Hill.

One final note: If there was ever any doubt that Jesse James had participated in the Hot Springs stage robbery, the question was surely put to rest when Jesse was shot and killed in St. Joseph, Missouri, eight years later. While searching through the dead outlaw's possessions, authorities found John Burbank's stolen watch. The recovered timepiece was eventually returned to Burbank, who was then living in Richmond, Indiana.[9]

CHAPTER 2

Flight Home to Missouri

If, as has been supposed, they were Missouri bushwhackers, they have already regained their haunts, and are now, most likely, planning another raid in some other direction.
—*Little Rock Republican,* January 30, 1874

After robbing the stagecoach, Jesse James and his accomplices mounted their horses and retreated back down the road toward Malvern. Their immediate aim was to distance themselves as far and as quickly as possible from the crime scene and from the posse they knew would surely come. Again crossing the Gulpha, the outlaws rode past the Gaines mansion and proceeded at a fast gallop until they came to Tiger Creek. At this small stream about six miles from the robbery site, they turned into the woods and rapidly headed north. The *Little Rock Republican* reported, "About a mile from where they left the main road they stopped, and evidently made a division of the spoils, for there were found there not only letters torn open, but also traces of a hasty bivouac. Some articles of clothing were also found at the spot, showing plainly that the highwaymen had changed a portion of their garments, in order to prevent detection, if possible."[1]

Sometime after dark, the fleeing bandits paused briefly at the home of a Mr. Houpt, whose farm was located on the old Benton stage road about fourteen miles from Hot Springs.

"There," according to the *Republican*, "they exchanged a worn out horse for a fresh one." Whether or not Mr. Houpt was a willing participant in that horse trade was not stated.

After proceeding a little farther, they stopped again—this time to rest. Evidence later showed that the outlaws built a fire and fed their animals before moving on. When next seen, they were riding past the home of a Mrs. Iron at the crossing of the upper Hot Springs road about twenty-four miles from the Springs.[2]

A gentleman identified only as J. J. Gillis gave this partial description of the fleeing robbers:

> One man five feet eight inches high, heavy, fair complexion, wide brim white hat, unshaved face for two weeks. One man five feet ten inches high, a brown soft high hat, very fair complexion, wore a moustache and had a dark nubia wrapped about his head. One man six feet high, with sandy whiskers, front teeth decayed, short whiskers over his face, and a black soft hat. All four [sic] had on water-proof leggins and three of them had on capes, the other wearing a blue coat. The chief of the gang wore a belt filled with cartridges. . . . They were all mounted on horses rather under size—one a sorrel with two white feet.[3]

At some point the fleeing horsemen crossed the Arkansas River and were later spotted in White County near the village of Beebe, thirty-some miles northeast of Little Rock. They continued to ride, and on the evening of January 19, five men answering the outlaws' descriptions stopped at the home of a Squire Lane. A few days after that visit, a letter from an unnamed White County farmer, presumably Mr. Lane, appeared in the *Little Rock Republican*. He wrote:

> It may be of some interest to you, to the public, and especially to the parties who were robbed on the Hot Springs stage, to know that a squad of five men, all of them on horseback, stopped all night at my house a few nights ago. They appeared to be in a hurry, as they did not arrive until after twilight on Monday evening and asked to have breakfast ready the next morning in time to be off by 6 o'clock, in order, they said, to get

to Jacksonport the same night. They professed to reside in Washington county, in this state. In their possession were two double-barreled shotguns, and my children say they all had revolvers also. Four of the party wore federal overcoats, and one had a gum-elastic overcoat—better known, probably, by the name of "water-proof." Two of them rode sorrel horses, one a black horse and one a pony; what the other man rode is not remembered. During their stay neither of them mentioned the name of any of the others.[4]

The men left the next morning before daylight. Lane's wife later said that after they mounted their horses, one of them appeared to put on a set of false whiskers.

It was now obvious that the stage robbers were retreating in a northeasterly direction basically following the Cairo and Fulton tracks. Reported sightings indicated they were traveling by way of the "bottom road," a course that, if maintained, would eventually take them across the White River at Peach Orchard Bluff, through the Cash Bottoms, and on into Southeast Missouri. The *Arkansas Gazette* commented, "From all appearances we should infer that these five men were the identical chaps that robbed the stage; if not, they were first cousins to them. The governor ought to offer a large reward, and station men to gobble them, on the route we have indicated."[5]

The newspaper's suggestion apparently went unheeded. Governor Baxter stationed no one along the escape route, and the stage robbers continued on their merry way, "ungobbled," through the flat, bottomland country of northeastern Arkansas. Several days after leaving the Lane residence, the horsemen were seen near Big Creek in Clayton County (now Clay County), not far from the Missouri border. The *Arkansas Gazette* reported:

> Five men passed through this county, coming from the direc-
> tion of Little Rock, and going in the direction of Dunklin
> county, Missouri. They stopped near here and took dinner, and
> said they were from Washington county, Ark., and had come by

way of Little Rock, but didn't know any citizen in Washington county, and would not tell where they were going. They all wore heavy government overcoats and furs around their necks. They had three shot-guns and some pistols; two or three gold watches and any amount of greenbacks. One of them was about six feet two inches high, light complexion and about forty years of age. Three others seemed to be about middle-aged men, medium-size, and one was a young man about twenty-five years old.

They were on good stock but it was much jaded. They swapped off one pony in this neighborhood, and gave eighty dollars difference for one that was fresh. They stopped nine miles above here on the Chalk Bluff road, and had their horses shod, and left there on Tuesday, the 27th, and went in the direction of Missouri.[6]

The stage robbers, moving free and easy across the Arkansas countryside, had now distanced themselves some two hundred miles from Hot Springs and were apparently no longer concerned about the possibility of capture. Tuesday, the same day they had their horses shod, the men "took dinner" at the little village of Moark near the state line.[7] After eating, they remounted, crossed into Missouri, and advanced northward along the tracks of the Iron Mountain Railroad.

In that part of Southeast Missouri the rail line passed through Neely's Swamp and a few small farm communities along the way. It is presumed that the outlaw gang followed the tracks north through or near Neelyville and Harviell and on up to Poplar Bluff by way of the Doniphan road. (According to a 1949 newspaper article, the outlaws stopped just south of the courthouse in Poplar Bluff at a small store owned by a man named Lacks. They bought some groceries, and after eating, one of them was supposed to have told Lacks: "If officers come by asking for the James gang, tell them we had lunch here." The men then rode away, leaving the grocer so upset he closed his store and went home.)[8]

The horsemen were now in the Ozark foothills of Butler County and gradually making their way to higher country. It was probably late Thursday, January 29, when they entered the county of Wayne.

Jack Myers told me of a stop the outlaws allegedly made at the home of his great-grandfather, John Larimore Miller, near Williamsville, Missouri. John's first wife, Evalina, had died nearly four years earlier leaving him with ten children, at least three of whom were still living at home. He had since remarried. The youngest of Evalina's children was little five-year-old Massie Batina Miller, Jack Myers' future grandmother. In later years Massie would tell Jack about the strangers who ate supper with her family that evening. Her stepmother, Mary, cooked the meal, and John let them spend the night in his barn. The next morning as they prepared to leave, one of the men took a coin from his pocket. "Here," he said, handing it to Massie, "you can tell people that Jesse James gave you a dime."[9]

The horsemen left the Williamsville area Friday morning and proceeded north some six miles to the small lumber town of Mill Spring. Hungry and perhaps in need of recreation, they stopped at McFadden's, a notorious gambling resort that, according to the *St. Louis Times*, bore "the reputation of being the rendezvous of the worst characters in Southeastern Missouri."[10] The newspaper claimed they spent the night at McFadden's, but it apparently erred because that afternoon, another six miles up the track, citizens of Piedmont reported seeing the men ride through their town. At that time, it was observed, "they wore federal overcoats, and all carried muskets."

Friday evening, about three miles above Piedmont, the weary travelers stopped at the home of a "Widow Gilbreath" and asked for food and a night's lodging. Mrs. Gilbreath invited them in and later said that when her visitors removed their overcoats, she noticed each was armed with two revolvers.[11] After breakfast the next morning they rode away. The widow was left with a few coins for her hospitality and, much more than that, an exciting story to tell her grandchildren. She had, after all, played hostess to a gentleman about whom stories and songs would one day be written—the legendary Missouri outlaw, Jesse James.

For now, though, the legend was still in the making. It was the morning of January 31, and Jesse and the boys were only four miles shy of their destination, Gads Hill. The ride from Hot Springs had been long and arduous, but they knew the worst was yet to come. That evening, according to plan, they would rob a railroad train and once again find themselves in "enemy territory." It was a situation with which the James and Younger brothers were all too familiar. They would take to the brush; the law would follow.

Dreading the long sleepless night of retreat that lay ahead, the outlaw band made final plans, studied maps, fed and groomed horses, checked ammunition, and cleaned weapons. After finishing these chores, there was little left to do but wait.

Meanwhile, in St. Louis, more than a hundred miles to the north, the Little Rock Express was taking on passengers and preparing to set out on its southward journey. Missouri's first train robbery was only hours away.

CHAPTER 3

The Express Heads South

On Saturday last I took the mail train of the St. Louis and Iron
Mountain Railroad for Poplar Bluff, where I was to hold a quarterly meeting. Under the management of T. McKissock, Esq.,
the gentlemanly and successful superintendent, the St. Louis
and Iron Mountain Railroad has come to be one of the most
pleasant and safe roads leading out of St. Louis. In its palace
cars, under the management of the courteous conductors, the
passengers are sure to have a pleasant journey in ordinary times.
—Portion of a letter from train passenger Rev. T. H. Hagerty
to the *St. Louis Globe* (printed February 4, 1874)

Train Number 7, the Little Rock Express, departed Plum Street
Station in St. Louis, Missouri, at 9:50 A.M. on that cold Saturday
morning, the last day of January.[1] Its destination: Little Rock,
Arkansas, 344 miles to the south. The steam locomotive, likely
a wood-burner, towed four cars: a combination mail-baggage-
express car, two regular passenger coaches, and a Pullman
sleeper.[2] There were eleven crewmen on board and a goodly
number of passengers.

In charge of this little procession was thirty-eight-year-old conductor Chauncey Alford, a popular, witty gentleman who had
served as conductor with the St. Louis and Iron Mountain
Railway for nine years—one-third of the time on passenger
trains. Alford, who stood six feet one inch tall, was described as

a quiet man, a man of nerve and common sense who had a humorous style of telling a story. He was regarded as "one of the safest men in the employ of the company."[3]

Besides the conductor, the crew on this particular run consisted of William Wetton, engineer; A. Campbell, fireman; O. Bennett and Ben Van Stumft, brakemen; Louis Constant, baggage man; William N. Wilson, express messenger; Mr. Marstan, mail agent; Alfred Butler, news agent; O. S. Newell, sleeping-car conductor; and the black porter, James Johnson. These men were assigned to run the train the first 185 miles—as far as the Arkansas state line. In Moark, Arkansas, they would be replaced by a fresh crew and return the following day to St. Louis on the northbound train from Little Rock.

The passengers, typically, came from various parts of the country and all walks of life. Their destinations were many, as were their reasons for making this trip. Some would be traveling only a few miles; others were bound for Little Rock; still others would switch trains in Little Rock and continue on to some other town or city. There were even a few adventurous souls going all the way to Texas, where the rail line had only recently been completed.

Aboard this day was Mrs. Scott of Pittsburgh, Pennsylvania, traveling with her young son to Hot Springs, Arkansas. This well-to-do lady had reason to be uneasy. She and the boy were scheduled to get off at Malvern and continue their journey to the Springs by stagecoach. They would be passing over the same road where just two weeks earlier a certain band of Missouri ruffians had stopped a westbound stage and robbed its passengers.

From Minnesota came two distinguished gentlemen—John F. Lincoln, superintendent of the St. Paul and Sioux City Railroad, and John L. Merriam, founder of the Merchants Bank of St. Paul. Merriam also owned a shipping and express business and was a member of the state legislature. His son, William, would later become Minnesota governor and, ironically, would hold that office during the incarceration of Cole, Jim, and Bob Younger in that state's penitentiary.

Rev. T. H. Hagerty (often mistakenly referred to by writers as "T. A. Hagbrit") was taking a 165-mile trip from St. Louis to

Poplar Bluff, Missouri, to hold a quarterly church meeting. He had traveled over the southern half of the state for the past ten years, he later said, "by rail, buggy, horse back and afoot," and until this day had never met with any serious problems.

In the seat facing the reverend sat a young St. Louis widow with her two small children, a boy and a girl. The three were on their way to her brother's home in Hot Springs and would be taking the same stagecoach as Mrs. Scott. Sitting with this little family was a Massachusetts woman bound for Texas to join her husband.

A lumber clerk, C. H. Henry, was going home to Clear Water, Missouri, to spend a few hours with his family. He would return to St. Louis by train the following day.

Also homebound was State Rep. L. M. Farris, traveling from the Missouri state capital, Jefferson City, to his farm in Reynolds County. His son would be meeting him with a team and wagon at Gads Hill, the station nearest his home.

Riding in the Pullman car were Col. and Mrs. James H. Morley of St. Louis. Colonel Morley was at that time chief engineer of the Cairo and Fulton Railroad, a subsidiary of the Iron Mountain Railway system. This prominent executive was the engineer who had some years earlier laid out and built the very road over which this little Iron Mountain train was now traveling. Morley's part of the road, completed April 2, 1858, ran from Plum Street Station in St. Louis eighty-six miles south to the village of Pilot Knob, where the terminus had remained until construction was resumed southward following the Civil War.[4] He and his wife were bound for Little Rock and, like their fellow travelers, were looking forward to getting this trip behind them.

Among others aboard the train were A. J. Merriman of Des Arc, Arkansas; J. H. Pearson of Little Rock; W. A. McClarren, a railroad conductor from Memphis; G. L. Dart of Peru, Indiana; and Silas Ferry of Hornellsville, New York. (The spellings of these and other passenger and town names often varied from one news account to the next.)

As the little caravan of cars rumbled slowly out of St. Louis, skirting the west bank of the Mississippi, passengers began to exchange pleasantries and become acquainted. Less sociable types entertained themselves by reading books or newspapers, or by watching the floating barges and steamboats working up and down the muddy river to their left. No one aboard the train had the slightest inkling that the notorious robber, Jesse James, and his band of bushwhackers were at that moment planning a most unpleasant reception a few hours down the line. Ignorance being bliss, the travelers settled back for what they had every reason to believe would be a safe and uneventful journey.

The train passed through the southside community of Carondelet and the historic military post, Jefferson Barracks, and after rolling along the river bluffs some twenty-five miles, departed the Mississippi for the open countryside. A short time later it made a brief stop in DeSoto and from that village continued southward into the ore-mining counties of Washington, St. Francois, and Iron. Including stops to take on fuel and pick up and put down passengers, the little "express" was averaging just over nineteen miles an hour.

By midafternoon the travelers had reached the beautiful Arcadia Valley in Iron County and were observing some of Missouri's most impressive Ozark hills. Iron Mountain, that magnificent ore-laden eminence for which the railroad was named, stood within two miles of the track. Nearby, too, was Pilot Knob Mountain, unique for its bald granite top and noted historically along with Shepherd Mountain as the site of a famous Civil War battle that had occurred less than a decade earlier.[5] Numerous other mountains and foothills also echoed the roar of the Little Rock Express as it slowly chugged its way south toward Arkansas.

There was much to see, but it was all starting to become somewhat repetitious to these rail-weary pilgrims. The piney-green mountains, wooded valleys, and clear flowing streams, scenic though they were, no longer held much interest. Boredom had set in some miles back and the only sights these good folks really wanted to see now were their respective destinations.

This boredom would soon be rudely interrupted.

CHAPTER 4

Gads Hill: "A Small Place, of No Account"

The station referred to is in Wayne county, about the center of one of the wildest and most unsettled districts through which any railroad in Missouri runs. On either hand of the line there are nothing but forest tracts with an occasional bridle path leading to nowhere, and at distant intervals a few farm houses, more noted for illicit distilling than the corn raised by the dwellers therein.

—*St. Louis Times*, February 1, 1874

When the Iron Mountain Railway opened its line south of Pilot Knob, Missouri, October 10, 1871, a number of little one-horse settlements quickly sprang up along the track. Surrounded by large expanses of pine and hardwood forest, most of the settlements in this particular section were created as centers for the timber industry. One of these was Gads Hill, situated at the crest of a long railroad grade in the Ozark wilderness of northwestern Wayne County, 120 rail miles south of St. Louis. This tiny hamlet owed its existence to Pekin Coal Company, which had established a cordwood and charcoal business there in November 1871, a month after the first regularly scheduled train rolled through. Platted by Piedmont, Missouri, hotel owner George W. Creath, it was named after the English country residence of the popular novelist Charles Dickens, who had recently died.

Dickens' home, near Gad's Hill, England, was known as Gad's Hill Place.[1]

(Interestingly, Gad's Hill, England, also claimed another literary distinction. A couple of centuries earlier, William Shakespeare had chosen it as the setting for a scene in his play *King Henry IV,* in which Sir John Falstaff and companions robbed a group of highway travelers. A possible connection between the Shakespearean drama and the Missouri train robbery will be briefly examined in a later chapter.)

At the time of our story, Gads Hill, Missouri, was barely breathing. Pekin had recently shut down its cordwood and charcoal operation, and the citizens who remained were eking out a meager living manufacturing "hoop poles."[2] Boasting a population of only fifteen or so people, the place consisted basically of three crude shanties, a small railroad platform, and the Pekin company store. The store also housed a post office, which served southern Iron County and a portion of northwestern Wayne County. There was no depot.[3] Just south of the platform a sidetrack, initially installed to accommodate the now idle sawmill, lay rusting. Stacks of lumber and a large sawdust pile stood as reminders of more prosperous times. To city dwellers passing through on the train, this little lost-in-the-forest settlement must have seemed like the edge of the world.

In railroad parlance Gads Hill was known as a "pick up and put down" station. That is, trains stopped only on those rare occasions when flagged by the station agent to allow a passenger to board, or upon orders from the conductor when someone was to get off. Ordinarily trains only slackened speed at the platform to exchange mail bags.[4] Conductor Alford referred to the settlement as "a small place, of no account," an opinion likely shared by many.

But regardless how unimpressive or no account this tiny backwoods whistle-stop might have been, it was about to become, for awhile at least, the most talked about place in the state. By playing host to Jesse James and Missouri's first train robbery this bleak winter day, January 31, 1874, little Gads Hill,

Old drawing entitled: "Nearing Gadshill." (Dacus)

Missouri, would not only experience a few brief moments of instant fame, but would have its name forever etched into the history of American outlawry.

Jesse and his friends had spent Friday night at Widow Gilbreath's, four miles south of Gads Hill, and left early Saturday morning. With hours to kill before the train was due and having made all necessary preparations for the robbery, they apparently decided to take a ride east toward Patterson, Missouri.

It is told that at midday they stopped for "dinner" at the home of Sarah Hamil, a widow with a large number of children. One of Sarah's daughters, sixteen-year-old Anna Belle Hamil, would later share her recollections of the outlaws' visit with her own children. During a tape-recorded interview in 1974, Anna's son Coker Montgomery, then seventy-eight, passed along his mother's story. It went like this.

The widow Sarah Hamil and her family were no doubt "having it pretty tough, but even at that, she wouldn't turn anybody away from her table," stated Montgomery. He continued:

Anna Belle Hamil Montgomery. As a sixteen-year-old girl she helped her widowed mother feed the outlaws. (Courtesy of Hamil Montgomery)

'Course that was the old Southern hospitality that she had. So these five men rode up there to the gate. Four of them come in . . . and left one man out at the gate with the horses . . . although the horses wasn't tied, not a one of them. But he stayed out there, I don't know, as a sentinel or what it could have been, but anyway he stayed out, and she fed the four and fixed dinner for the fifth one.

Young Anna probably helped with the cooking and may have taken the plate of food to the sentinel. In telling the story to her son years later, she recalled that the saddle horses ridden by the strangers were the finest she had ever seen.

"When they got through eating," Montgomery told the interviewer, "each man left a five-dollar gold piece at his plate—except this one particular man, which was supposed to have been Jesse James. He left a ten." That was to pay for himself and the man who stayed with the horses, Montgomery explained, "but it was five dollars a meal that they give, which was an unheard-of price at that time."[5]

Leaving Sarah, Anna, and the children with that extremely generous sum, the men mounted their horses and rode away, presumably down the Peach Tree road in the direction of that "small place, of no account"—Gads Hill.

PART II

The Robbery

Thomas Purrington Fitz, station agent at Gads Hill. (Courtesy of Alice Fitz White)

CHAPTER 5

Unwelcome Guests

But my lads, my lads . . . at Gad's Hill! There are pilgrims going to Canterbury with rich offerings, and traders riding to London with fat purses. I have vizards for you all; you have horses for yourselves. . . . If you will go, I will stuff your purses full of crowns.

—William Shakespeare, *King Henry IV*, Part I, Act I, Scene 2

It was only midafternoon in the Missouri Ozarks, but seemed much later. The winter sun, already low in the western sky, was hardly visible through the haze. Wood smoke from cabin chimneys lay heavy in surrounding valleys—to hillfolk a sure sign of approaching bad weather. Smoke rising meant fair weather; smoke riding low meant bad. It would surely snow before morning, they thought.

Gads Hill was quiet—awake, but not noticeably. Chickens wandered about scratching among the leaves and pine needles for edible morsels. A couple of coonhounds, too stupid to be cold, lounged lazily on the porch of the Pekin store, and a wagon team and a few saddle horses stood tethered to nearby saplings. Inside the store several male citizens were sitting around the old potbelly stove spinning yarns, whittling, chawing, and discussing affairs of the day. Now and then someone would get up to poke the fire and toss in another log or step outside to check the weather. That was about as exciting as things got on a Saturday at Gads Hill—except, of course, for that brief moment, twice daily, when an Iron Mountain train would rumble through and drop off the mail bags. Nothing much ever topped that, not around there anyway.

The northbound had passed some hours earlier on its way to St. Louis. The southbound from St. Louis to Little Rock, if on time, would be rolling in at 4:06 P.M. Today the southbound was expected to make one of its rare stops to let off a passenger—State Rep. L. M. Farris of Reynolds County.

Among the store's occupants was the station agent, Thomas P. Fitz, of nearby Des Arc, Missouri. During the war this thirty-three-year-old native of Albemarle County, Virginia, had served with the First Virginia Artillery and later with the Fifth Virginia Cavalry under Gen. Fitzhugh Lee. He had taken part in major battles from Yorktown to Appomattox, including the Battle of Gettysburg. Thankfully, though, that was all in the past. Tom had moved to Missouri back in 1867, and today as he sat quietly at his railroad job, relaxing with friends and neighbors in the little country store at Gads Hill, the horrors of war seemed a lifetime ago. America was at peace, and so was Tom.[1]

Another who shared the warmth of fire and friendship this day was sixteen-year-old Billy Farris. Billy had just arrived from the Farris farm, six miles west of Gads Hill, to meet his father's train. He was early. The express was not due for another hour.

The storekeeper, Mr. McMillen, was also present in the group and there were three or four others. One of these was said to have been Billy's young friend, Joe Wiggens. Another was supposedly Frank Carter, owner of one of the saddle horses tied out front.[2]

As the men and boys sat warming themselves inside the store, things were starting to heat up outside as well. Those five armed strangers who had been seen near Patterson earlier in the day were at that moment riding down the road in their direction. Only one of the horsemen was now wearing his overcoat. The others had evidently shed theirs for the business at hand. All wore hats, according to a witness, and were dressed in plain homespun clothing and long cavalry leggings. The men were masked with white shoulder-length hoods, each held in place by a "long scarf wrapped around the neck and tied turbanlike over the head." Eyeholes were cut, triangular in shape, with the bases at the eyebrows and the points downward along the cheeks. At least one mask had a mouth hole. They carried a small arsenal, in full view, each man being armed with several splendid navy revolvers, "silver mounted," it was said, "with ivory handles." Three had double-barreled shotguns.[3] These fellows did not appear to be dropping by for tea.

The first to spot the approaching horsemen was a group of children playing by the roadside. One of the smaller boys was Ami Dean (known in adult life as M. I. Dean). Dean is remembered by those who knew him in Mill Spring in the 1930s and 1940s as an elderly man, partially crippled, who worked as custodian for the local school; he was also employed part time at the Mill Spring depot, where he hung mail for train pickup. Dean used to recall that when he saw the masked strangers riding toward him that day in 1874, he became terribly frightened and ran crying for home. Apparently trying to ease his fears, one of the men called out, "Don't be afraid, little boy! We won't hurt you!" Needless to say, young Ami found little comfort in those words and didn't stop running until he was home safe in his mother's arms.[4]

As the sinister-looking bunch entered Gads Hill, chickens scattered, dogs began to bark, and folks stared from windows. Dismounting, the men tethered their horses to a cluster of saplings some distance from the track and proceeded to hammer on doors, rousting all residents from their homes. The men and boys were marched out of the store to a spot near the railroad platform where they were forced to build a large bonfire. There the villagefolk—men, women, and children—huddled to keep warm, all the while under the watchful eye of one or more of their armed abductors.

Gads Hill as it appeared in the late 1940s. This view looks east down the Peach Tree road, supposedly the route by which the train bandits approached the village in 1874. At left is the railroad station (built some years after the robbery) and the old tree where legend claimed Jesse James tied his horse. (Illustration by author)

In this early 1960s photograph, the legendary "Jesse James tree" casts its shadow on the former railroad station, then being used as a mission. The tree, building, and Peach Tree road have long since disappeared from the scene. (Courtesy of the Daily American Republic, *Poplar Bluff, Missouri)*

The only person robbed at that time was McMillen, the store-keeper, a gentleman who obviously didn't believe in banks. His pockets were picked of a reported $700 or $800. Fortunately, however, the robbers overlooked $450 that had slipped down in the lining of his coat. McMillen also lost a rifle to the bandits.[5]

Having secured the village, the masked intruders collared a citizen (Tom Fitz probably) and demanded the key to the railroad switches. He didn't have it, he said, nor did anyone else in the village. A young man named W. H. Colman was the keeper of the key, and he had been called away that morning to his job at Clear Water. The key was in his pocket.[6] Accepting that explanation, the outlaws ignored the locks and with a two-by-four pried open the switches, north and south. Their plan was simple. The open north switch would divert the incoming train onto the sidetrack, and the open south switch would force the engineer to stop to avoid derailment. Once in place the train would be helplessly locked on the siding, unable to go forward or back. It was hard work, and at some point the man wearing the Federal overcoat removed it and laid it on the tracks. When his task was finished, he left the garment there and returned to the bonfire. Another man planted a red signal flag near the platform. This done, the trap was set. All the outlaws needed now was a train. They would have a much longer wait than anticipated.

Meanwhile, a few miles up the track, the Little Rock Express was rocking along on schedule and drawing ever nearer to its date with destiny. It passed through the small villages (some of which no longer exist) of Arcadia, Hogan Mountain, Russell's Mill, Ozark Mills, and Annapolis and at about 3:50 P.M. pulled into Des Arc, the station just north of Gads Hill. Here, the train met with an unexpected delay. Most of the little town's 100 inhabitants were at that moment outside working frantically to extinguish a fire that had somehow started in a carload of cotton off the main track. Alford volunteered his train crew to help, and with Rev. T. H. Hagerty and another passenger or two joining in, it was eventually brought under control. As soon as all parties were back on board, Alford signaled the engineer and the journey resumed.

The excitement of the Des Arc fire was soon forgotten, and things returned to normal. Moments later, the train, running now about forty minutes late, was chugging up a certain six-mile grade in Wayne County. The passengers yawned wearily as conductor Alford announced:

"Next stop—Gads Hill!"

CHAPTER 6

Capture of the Little Rock Express

A man advanced and caught me by the collar and stuck a pistol in my face. . . . I was a little surprised, but understood his object when he shouted . . . "Stand still or I'll blow the top of your head off." He at the same time yelled out: "If a shot is fired out of the car I will kill the conductor."
—Conductor Chauncey Alford, *Chicago Tribune*,
February 4, 1874

As the approaching train slowly made its way up the grade, the masked men took their assigned positions. Three of them crawled under the station platform, another hid on the opposite side of the track, and the fifth man stood in full view on the platform. Billy Farris and the villagers, still uncomfortably within shotgun range of their captors, remained at the bonfire. Aboard the train, Representative Farris was busy gathering his carpetbags as he prepared to debark. Conductor Alford glanced at his watch. The time was 4:45 P.M.

The moment the train topped the grade, engineer Bill Wetton knew something was terribly wrong. Looking ahead to the village, he saw a crowd of men, women, and children huddled around a large bonfire. He also noticed that the sidetrack had been opened, and, even more alarming, there was someone standing on the station platform waving a red flag. To a railroad man a red flag signal means only one thing—danger ahead on the track. Already running the train at reduced speed, Wetton did not entirely shut off steam, and the train slowly switched off the main track onto the siding.

Conductor Alford later told a reporter, "On approaching the station, the engineer signaled by whistling to 'brake,' as danger was ahead; on going out upon the platform of one of the cars, and looking forward over the side, I saw a red flag being violently waved by a masked man; I jumped off the car and ran ahead to inquire about the cause of such a demonstration." Alford said that he jumped off before the train had fully stopped because he thought the track might be torn up and they were about to derail. "As I struck the platform," he stated, "I noticed the train running on the side track. The northern switch had been opened and so had the southern, and when we got on the side track we were stuck, for had we started forward or back, we would have run off the track."

Alford said at first he saw only one man, "the same one that had the flag." Then, according to his testimony, "on my approaching this man, three masked men crawled from under the station platform; another masked man appeared upon the opposite side of the track; two of the men seized me by the coat collar and asked me if I was the conductor; I told them I was; they then told me to keep still and I would not be hurt."

The conductor now stood facing the unfriendly muzzle of a cocked navy revolver. Its owner spoke in a "hoarse voice" and was described by Alford as a "huge six footer [whose] face was covered with a mask made of white cloth, with holes cut for his eyes and mouth." When a reporter asked if he had been frightened by this sudden confrontation with the masked gunman, Alford replied in his own humorous style, "Well, I reckon I was somewhat frightened; but he put me right at my ease—he comforted me."

What did he say?

"'Stand still, or I'll blow the top of your d——d head off.'"

"I stood still," Alford added.

Glancing around, the conductor made a quick assessment of the situation:

> A number of persons were on the platform under guard, and it was ascertained that all the residents of the place, including boys and girls, had been captured. They were gathered about a fire in the open air to keep them warm. It turned out that the place was in possession of five desperadoes, three of whom were armed with double-barrel guns, and all had navy revolvers.

Two of the men rushed forward and at gunpoint forced engineer Wetton and fireman Campbell off the locomotive. Alford continued his story. "Some of the passengers and trainmen rushed out upon the platforms, and others put their heads out of the windows, to see what the trouble was; the fifth masked man ran along the side of the cars, and with a pistol in each hand, shouting that myself and the engineer were held as hostages for the passengers' good behavior, and if any one attempted to fire we would be shot; in a few minutes the engineer, fireman, brakemen, and myself were placed upon the station platform with a guard of two of the gang over us; the guards held large navy revolvers to our heads and took our pistols, watches, etc."

Alford said that one of the men went to the opposite side of the train and, "as the passengers put their heads out, he told them to take those heads back again or they'd lose 'em." Alford added, "He had a double-barreled shotgun, and I don't think he was fooling any."[1]

Rev. T. H. Hagerty also had a story, which he later told in a letter to the *St. Louis Globe*. At the time the express pulled into Gads Hill, he was sitting comfortably in his coach reading a book. He glanced out the window. Everything seemed normal. "The whistle sounded," he wrote, "the bell rung, the train stopped as usual, at least so far as any of us passengers knew." But then things started to happen.

I looked out on the right of the road and saw a team hitched to a tree being extremely restive, and just then I saw a man coming on the fast run, behind and parallel to the train, and, as I supposed, running to save his team; but instead of stopping at the team he hastened forward, coming toward the train. I then for the first observed that he was masked, and had a gun in his hand. I then raised the window and looked out of the left hand side, and saw a bonfire and a crowd of men and boys about it. Next I saw our gentlemanly conductor standing on the platform, and a masked man at his side holding a pistol to his head and talking most boisterously. The facts then flashed upon me in a moment. I went to the door and looked out, and saw several masked persons about the front of the train, with a great commotion and horrid oaths and commands of "Stand still!" "Go back into the cars!" "Keep your seats!" "Shoot the first man that stirs!" As I learned the robbers had opened the switch and run the train in, and opened the switch in the rear and forward both. They took the engineer from his engine, and gave orders to shoot the first man that attempted to advance toward it. The train was now stopped, and we were at the mercy of five men whom we did not know, and did not know how long we would know them or any other of our *friends*. Seeing the situation as I stood upon the platform, and hearing the stern and oath-accompanied commands, I thought I would obey, at least when they did not ask anything harder of me than to go back into the car. I always want to live ready for a departure for the better world, but I did not see just then that these gentlemen were the proper ones to invite me to take that journey.

Hagerty returned to his seat and with his fellow passengers sat down to await whatever fate had in store. "I, of course, prayed," the reverend wrote, "as I always do, for direction and preservation."[2]

Another man who had an interesting story to tell was Adams Express messenger Bill Wilson. He recalled:

As the train came to a halt, I heard someone making a noise on the platform, and looking out I saw a man strutting about; I saw he was armed, but thought he was drunk, and took my seat again. Presently, I heard an unusual noise, heard voices using terrible threats and oaths, and on looking out on the opposite side of the car, saw two men armed with pistols and guns. I also noticed that they were both masked. I afterwards discovered the man I first seen was masked, but I did not observe it at first; I thought he was drunk and paid little attention to him. But as soon as I saw the masked men the truth flashed on me. I knew we were being robbed.[3]

Realizing the situation, Wilson decided to take action. "I had no idea how many of the robbers there might be," he said, "but I had a pistol in the safe, and getting it, I determined to protect the property under my charge." With pistol in hand he waited.

Meanwhile, outside, Billy Farris saw his father preparing to exit the train and ran to him. Shouting that a holdup was in progress, he instructed him to get off on the side where the villagers were. Mr. Farris did so and was not robbed.[4]

In later years, Billy was said to have told his part a bit differently. For this story we turn to a 1948 newspaper clipping featuring an interview with a man named Dave Miller. When Miller was a boy, he said, the aging Billy Farris lived for awhile with him and his family near Riverside (a tiny community near the robbery site) and used to delight neighborhood children with tales of his Gads Hill experience. Miller claimed he heard old Billy tell the story this way: After being marched outside the store, Billy and Frank Carter were ordered to stack some loose railroad ties onto the track. Shortly after finishing this chore, they heard the train coming. According to the article, Jesse James quickly pulled a red flag from his pocket and, handing it to Billy, told him to run up the tracks about a hundred yards or so and stop the train. If the boy refused, or tried anything out of the ordinary, the gunman cautioned, he would be shot. Billy did as he was told, but, after flagging down the train, he ignored the outlaws' weapons and brazenly climbed aboard to warn the unsuspecting passengers about what was happening. Billy said he never knew why Jesse didn't shoot him; he supposed it was because he was just a kid, and Jesse James was not a murderer.[5]

If young Farris did indeed flag down and board the Little Rock Express that day, it was not reported in contemporary newspapers. Nor was there any mention of cross-ties being placed on the tracks. Perhaps those parts of the story were little details "remembered" years later in the retelling.

In any case, when the train stopped and Mr. Farris stepped down, he was immediately confronted by one of the gunmen. The *Little Rock Republican*, with a slant toward humor and probably exaggerating just a bit, gave this account:

> A laughable incident is told in connection with a member of the lower house of the Missouri legislature who jumped off the train as it stopped, Gads Hill being the nearest station to his home. Seeing the commotion, the fire and the grouped inhabitants, he struck an oratorical pose, and cried out in a rotund legislative accent: "What in hell is the matter now?" The polite bandit on guard at the fire responded and leveled his fowling-piece at the same time: "Come here you sweet-scented son of a —— and warm yourself. Come, hurry, I want to look at you." He went, and soon felt warmer than he thought was healthful.[6]

During the time he was held hostage, the congenial Mr. Farris talked freely with the guard, whom he later described as "a tall, heavy set, dark-skinned man with a coarse voice." This was undoubtedly the same "huge six footer" who had collared conductor Alford. Farris was later interviewed at his office in Jefferson City and offered more information about his captor:

> This guard, like the others, was very merry and talkative. He said they had been well raised but had been ill treated, had fallen from grace and been driven to this mode of livelihood. They wanted a little change and if the citizens would keep quiet no one would be hurt.

At some point during the proceedings, engineer Wetton asked the guard if he might be allowed to get back on the engine, "that she was getting on too much steam." The guard apparently did not share Wetton's concern. "Let her bust," he was quoted as saying. "But," he added, "we'll try to get away before she does."[7]

Conductor Alford later recalled that four of the masked men "were tall and slim, about six feet high; the other . . . was a heavy set man of about five feet eight inches." Typically, though, eyewitness descriptions varied. Mr. Farris said that only two were six feet, the others not as tall. The shortest of the five, he noticed, "had one or two under teeth out," and through their masks he was somehow able to observe that two of the robbers "looked like brothers, with fair skin and blue eyes." But whatever their appearance, these gun-wielding men in masks were not pretty to look at and caused considerable apprehension among the passengers.

In contrast to the uneasiness felt by those on the train, the citizens of Gads Hill had by this time apparently become somewhat bored with their captivity. It was later told that some of them actually stretched out by the fire and went to sleep, or pretended to. According to one report, when the robbery finally got under way, the villagers were locked up in one of the houses.[8]

Everything was going as planned. The marauders had taken control of the village, had succeeded in maneuvering the train onto the siding, and had forced the passengers and crew to surrender—all without firing a shot. With two men standing guard outside the train threatening to shoot anyone who stepped off or showed resistance, the remaining three climbed aboard. The leader of this masked trio, as we will later see, was probably Frank James.

CHAPTER 7

"Robbed at Gads Hill"

It's all right, send for the detectives; before they can get here
we'll be 500 miles away.
—Outlaw to express messenger William N. Wilson,
St. Louis Dispatch, February 5, 1874

Entering first the mail-baggage-express car, the three masked
men quickly overpowered mail agent Marstan and baggage
man Louis Constant. The robbers were unaware that a third
trainman, Bill Wilson, was waiting for them in another compartment of the car, armed. Marstan and Constant were forced
into a corner and guarded "at the point of a frightful looking
pistol." When Marstan was slow in pointing out the registered
mail, the intruders began helping themselves, tearing open
packages until they found what they wanted.

After this pilferage, two of the outlaws temporarily left the
car to escort Marstan and Constant to the platform, where conductor Alford and several other crewmen were being guarded.
It was here that one of the robbers relieved Alford of his fine
gold watch, a gift he had recently received from friends. This
got an immediate response from Constant. "For God's sake,"
he reportedly said, "don't take his watch; it was a present to
him." The "captain" of the outlaws, as conductor Alford called
him, ordered it returned. "They seemed to be under the control of the captain," he later stated, "and gave the watch back

A portion of the old Iron Mountain railroad grade as it appears today just north of Gads Hill. The robbery site lies beyond the trees in the upper right.

to me." Alford was also fleeced of fifty dollars, which they did not return.[1]

Louis Constant was apparently a nervy cuss and not as cooperative as the bandits would have liked. Because of this they treated him somewhat roughly, poking him repeatedly in the ribs with their revolvers. Constant, who was described as "a large, fleshy man," later joked that as a result of the poking "his clothes were entirely too big for him for two days after the robbery."

Having delivered Constant and Marstan to the platform, the two holdup men then started back to rejoin their companion, who was continuing to rummage through the registered mail. The outlaw thought he was alone in the car, but of course he was not. At the far end, waiting silently and nervously in the express compartment, stood Bill Wilson, still clutching his pistol. Wilson later described the confrontation:

> The car I was on had three departments, one for the mail, one for the baggage, and the other used by the Adams Express Company. I fastened the door in my end of the car, and took a position facing the door leading from the baggage department of the car. I heard the guards swearing and threatening to shoot anyone who poked his head out of a car. I had waited but a short time when one of the robbers appeared at the door leading into my department. He had his hands filled with registered letters. I pointed my pistol at him and told him to "drop those letters," which he did instantly. At this time two more robbers entered the car by the side doors and, pointing their guns at me, told me to "drop that pistol." I dropped it, or rather handed it to the one that reached for it.
>
> The man who had dropped the letters put a pistol in my face and said, "You was going to shoot me, was you? I've a notion to blow the top of your head off."[2]

The outlaws then ordered Wilson off the train, but immediately called him back and asked for the keys to the express safe. "I offered them to one of the men," Wilson said, "but they made me unlock the safe and take out the packages."

Some of the packages contained money; some contained bills and drafts. The outlaws made it clear that they were not interested in the latter. "We want money," one of them demanded, "or something that can be turned into money in a hurry."

As Wilson separated the express packages, a robber stood over him watching his every move. In one instance he attempted to fool the overseer by putting a $500 package with the drafts and calling out "draft," but the robber was too sharp for him. "Hello, my friend," he was quoted as saying, "you can't come that game on me. Let me have that package—$500, eh?"

Wilson told a reporter, "After getting all the money packages and the registered letters, the robbers wanted to be shown other valuables in the car and began to break open some of the baggage, but I begged them not to do it, that they would find nothing of any value to them." They seemed to agree and spent little time there. The only items taken from the baggage compartment were some tobacco and a pistol pilfered from conductor Alford's valise.

When the bandits were at last satisfied that they had "cleaned out" the car, as one of them put it, two of the men stepped off, leaving Wilson alone with the third. Wilson later recalled the conversation with his captor.

"I have always been in the habit," he told the outlaw, "of having people sign a receipt when I deliver them packages."

"Oh, well," answered the masked man, "just hand me your book and I'll sign."

Wilson handed over the receipt book and, flipping to an appropriate page, the outlaw facetiously wrote, "Robbed."[3] (Conductor Alford, in his version of the story, stated that the man wrote, "Robbed at Gads Hill.")[4]

Laying the pen down, the gunman said, "There it is, and it's not the first time I've signed in your book."

"Where did you ever sign in my book before?" Wilson wanted to know.

"You never mind about that," was the answer.

Wilson closed the receipt book and returned it to its place on the shelf.

"I know you," the outlaw continued, "and you are the only man on this train I fear."

"Why do you fear me?" asked Wilson.

"I fear you will give information to the detectives," he replied. "But, it's all right, send for the detectives; before they can get here we'll be 500 miles away."[5]

After finishing this bit of small talk, the masked man shoved his revolver in Wilson's back and marched him to the station platform, where he was placed under guard along with his fellow trainmen.

Although he had been robbed and his life had been threatened, Wilson later spoke well of his abductors. When asked what kind of men they seemed to be, he responded, "They acted rather gentlemanly, considering what they were doing, and talked like men of some intelligence."

Gentlemanly though they might have been, the robbers left the ransacked car a mess. Torn envelopes, letters, and receipts and broken packages littered the floor. Most of the letters, it was said, were "so badly torn and mutilated that their full addresses could not be found, and a few were so tramped upon and soiled that it was with difficulty the inscriptions could be deciphered." The amount stolen from the mail compartment was never fully reported, although one of the registered packages was known to have been looted of $2,000. The post office in St. Louis later announced that about thirty registered letters had been on the train, nearly all containing money or money orders. Only four were actually taken, however.

Conductor Alford reported that Adams Express Company lost $1,080 in the robbery; other reports varied slightly from that figure. One account gave the figure as $1,103.80, of which $41.05 belonged to express messenger Wilson.[6]

Still lusting for greenbacks, the outlaws then turned their attention to the passenger cars.

CHAPTER 8

The Robin Hood Image Upheld

The robbers examined the hands of the male passengers, and if found hard they were let off without being robbed, but if found to be soft they were invariably plundered.
—Passenger C. H. Henry, *St. Louis Times,* February 2, 1874

Conductor Alford said that at the time of the robbery there were twenty-five passengers aboard the train—twelve men, five women, and eight children. Along with the eleven crewmen and the citizens of Gads Hill, the outlaw band was outnumbered ten to one, but of course the threatening pistols and shotguns of the outlaws made those odds rather meaningless.

With a guard still in place on either side of the train, the three robbers stepped aboard the smoking car. Here, the passengers, all male, were told to sit still and no one would be hurt. The gunmen stated that "they were only after the 'sons of ———' with plug hats, and did not desire to molest or rob workingmen or those who earned their bread with the sweat of their brows."[1] One of the passengers in this car was J. H. Pearson, a resident of Little Rock. Pearson must have been wearing a plug hat, because he was forced to fork over seven dollars.[2]

Apparently the plug hats were not their only target. It seems they were not overly fond of Yankees either. The *St. Louis Democrat* reported, "The robbers boasted of their Southern proclivities, and damned all who acknowledged themselves Northern men, and called them such pet names as black-guards and pimps [in their] address to each other. They did not care about going for anybody but G—d—— Yankees, unless the d——d fools from elsewhere wore plug hats."[3]

Meanwhile, ahead in the first-class coach, the more affluent passengers waited. They knew the thieves would soon come calling, and some of them used the time wisely by trying to find creative ways of hiding their worldly goods. Hagerty later wrote:

> Most if not all of the gentlemen got up and excitedly felt for their pockets, and for some reason a number of them had occasion to pull up their pantlegs and adjust their boots. Others found their seats were not just as they liked, and turned them up and then readjusted them. Others took off their watches, some were thrown under the seat, one in the wood-box, one behind the zinc lining back of the stove.

As for the reverend, he made no attempt to conceal any of his possessions. He wrote, "I did not move a thing of mine, nor stir from my seat after I came back from the first look-out. My watch, what little money I had and satchel remained with me just as they were, and I proposed to abide the result."

Hearts surely beat fast during this time, but according to Hagerty, one "good-natured Irishman" (whose pocket flask of spirits no doubt contributed much to his good nature) seemed unruffled by it all. Plopping himself down across from the reverend and putting his feet up on the seat before him, he leaned back and said to his fellow passengers, "Gentlemen and ladies, just be quiet, and they will not hurt one of us."

Aboard this coach were three women, two of whom sat facing the reverend. One was traveling alone, the other with two small children. As the wait continued, recalled Hagerty, one of the children, a little six-year-old boy, looked up at his mother and asked with wide-eyed innocence, "Ma, where are the police?"

The police didn't come, but the outlaws did. Entering the car and flashing their revolvers, one of them announced that they were robbers and wanted money. "Keep your seats," he said, "or we will shoot the first —— one that moves! Men, have you any arms? If so, give them up!"

Hagerty described the intruders:

> Their masks were thin cotton cloth drawn over their faces and under their chins, tied back of their necks. They all had hats on. Holes were cut out for the eyes in the shape of a cone, the base being at the eyebrows and the point down beside the nose. There was no hole for the mouth, and breathing through the cloth dampened it, which soon collected dust, causing it to look black. They were not by any means good-looking in their outfits. I wonder the ladies did not scream or swoon away. Their revolvers were fine, large new ones; most all of them had three—sometimes one in each hand, or one in the right hand and two in the belt.

Armed as the robbers were and threatening violence, it is a wonder that even some of the male passengers didn't "scream or swoon away." However, most remained calm—outwardly, at least. Hagerty later praised the "cool manner" of the train crew, Chauncey Alford in particular. He wrote, "If the conductor, Mr. Alford, had got excited and beside himself, and acted wildly, we might all, or most of us, have been slaughtered; he, like General Grant, stood there and puffed away at his cigar, very coolly."

The reverend told what the masked men did next:

> Two of them then walked the entire length of the coach, to see, I suppose, that the coast was clear, and then commenced the work in detail. They would accost one man thus: "Who are you, sir? Where are you from? What is your business? Well, I will take your money!" a pistol or two being held at his head all the while. Some would take out their money (from $3 to $173) and hand it to them. "Is that all you have got?" If a small amount, sometimes they would throw it back and say: "You can keep that," or they would say of a larger amount, "You can spare me that." Sometimes they would search his pockets and his person, and

> sometimes they would turn up the seat of the car; other times
> they would make him open his satchel. Upon other occasions
> they would open them themselves. They did not appear to have
> their plans well matured, but acted upon the spur of the
> moment.[4]

Assuring their captives that they had no intention of robbing workingmen or ladies, the thieves proceeded to examine the palms of the male passengers. Those whose hands were found to be callous were not robbed, but those whose hands were soft were plundered without hesitation. When passenger C. H. Henry asked why this was being done, one of the outlaws responded, "Hard-handed men have to work for their money, while the soft-handed ones are capitalists, professors, and others that get money easy."[5] Soft-handed Mr. Henry was relieved of $154. He was allowed to keep his silver watch but not as an act of kindness. Silver watches were just not up to the outlaws' standards and in all instances were returned to their owners.

Hagerty observed:

> Sometimes they would approach a man and accost him with
> "Show me your hands, sir. Well, sir, you looked as though you
> worked for your living, we don't want your money;" or "Well, sir,
> you have an easy time of it. I will take your money, if you please,
> sir. Come, hurry up, don't be so slow about it, we are in a d——
> hurry." Sometimes they would say "Let me see your watch, sir."
> They would look at it and hand it back, saying "You can keep it,
> I don't want it." They took the conductor's $200 watch, and he
> said, "I wish you would let me keep that, it was a present to me."
> They handed it back. They only took one watch from our coach,
> but the man came back and said, "Are you the man I got this
> watch from?" "Yes, sir." "Well, you can have it, I don't want it."
> The gentleman took the watch and thanked him.

Hagerty was seated in the middle of the coach and had considerable time to think over his situation before the three robbers got to him. He recalled:

> When they began to inquire for men's names and occupations,
> I was in a query to know how my name and occupation would

pass among these gentlemen of masked faces. But as I could do no better, I thought I would "face the music" boldly. Just before they got to me they got to asking men to show their hands, and a number had passed on that test. I then thought, "Good luck for me." At the last station a car of cotton had caught fire, and I worked in the mud and water for about an hour, to assist in putting it out, and got my face flushed up and hands dirty and considerably covered with mud. I wanted to stop at the brook and wash up, but the conductor said that I would not have time. I thought that the burning cotton, the conductor and Providence, without my knowing it, had prepared a smooth-handed preacher to "pass muster" under a pistol, where I never was before.

The preacher recounted his conversation with the outlaw he perceived to be in charge:

When the chief came to me, he said, muddy as I was: "Well, who are you?" Did not ask anything about my hands. I, however, by the blessing of God, was ready with an answer, "I am a minister, sir!" "Oh, well we don't want to disturb you! Boys, don't molest this minister; we will let him pass." "Stop a moment, my friend," I said. "I would like to pray with you boys." "No, never mind now; we hain't time." "Have you a mother?" I asked. "Yes sir," said the chief. "Does she pray?" I asked. "Yes sir, and a good one," he said. "Well, I hope you will remember her instruction," I said. He answered, "You pray for us to-night, and I hope your prayers will be answered in our behalf, and that we all may get to the good country."[6]

(Perhaps Hagerty interpreted "the good country" as a metaphor for heaven, and that may indeed have been the outlaw's meaning, but it would seem more likely that the outlaw was referring to western Missouri, where he and his gang had friends and relatives who would hide them from the law.)

The robbers took nothing from the preacher nor from the women passengers who sat facing him. They were, in fact, most courteous. Upon passing they turned, bowed politely, and said, "Don't be alarmed, ladies, we will not disturb you." The ladies breathed much freer after that, wrote Hagerty, "and I for them."

Although Hagerty was not fond of the way the robbers expressed themselves, he gave them high marks for their general behavior. He wrote:

> Except in the use of rough and profane language, the men acted as gentlemanly as they could in their line of business. They did not appear disposed to destroy anything nor to molest anything, but simply to get a few greenbacks to help them along these hard times. They appeared in good clothing, and their language was not the boorish language heard among dishonest men.

Hagerty's views were apparently shared by other passengers. The *Little Rock Republican* reported:

> All parties on the train unite in expressing the opinion that the bandits were not only cool and deliberate knaves, but, considering their purpose and profession, extremely polite and gentlemanly ones. They made no threats toward any one beyond a gentle reminder that resistance would be death, and an occasional close application of a revolver to the cranium of a slow producer of greenbacks and watches. They kindly assured the ladies that no harm would come to them, and gently patted on the head one or two children on the train by way of expressing their admiration for innocence.[7]

Across from Hagerty sat the Irishman, patiently awaiting his turn. This son of the old sod may have been W. A. McClarren,[8] a passenger who was reportedly fleeced of $15, a finger ring worth $30, and a breast pin valued at $100. After they "got through with the good-natured Irishman," as Hagerty put it, he took out his pocket flask and asked, "Won't you have a drink, boys?" The offer was declined. "No sir. I am afraid you might have it spiked," the chief joked.

Proceeding down the aisle, the trio approached a woman who had what was described as "a magnificent gold watch and chain." They allowed her to keep it, but one of them did relieve her of three fancy pocket handkerchiefs, items that no doubt later became presents for a wife, girlfriend, or mother.

During the course of the robbery, the three men repeatedly

asked for "Mr. Pinkerton," whom they somehow supposed was on the train.[9] They were, of course, referring to none other than Allan Pinkerton, head of the Chicago-based Pinkerton National Detective Agency. The James-Younger gang hated detectives even more than they hated Yankees and wearers of plug hats, and first and foremost on their list of the despicable was Allan Pinkerton. In 1861, during the Civil War, Mr. Pinkerton had been appointed by President Lincoln to head a secret service organization to spy for the Union Army. Now, in charge of his own private detective agency, this renowned sleuth had many civilian successes to his credit—among them, the capture of America's first train-robbing gang, the Reno brothers.[10] Since June 1871, the Pinkerton force had been after Jesse James and his band.[11]

Getting no answer to their inquiries, the three gunmen began to suspect various individuals of being the famous detective. In two separate incidents, male passengers in Hagerty's coach were suspected and "approached quite roughly." To one the outlaw leader reportedly growled, "If you are the man I think you are I will end your days right here, on the spot!" After examining the gentleman's papers, the gunmen realized they were mistaken and moved on. Fortunately for the man he was not Mr. Pinkerton; and fortunately for Mr. Pinkerton he was not aboard the train.

Having plundered this car, the trio advanced toward the door leading to the Pullman. Hagerty recalled:

> I saw one of [the robbers] take a bundle of bills out of his pocket as large as his double-fists, and readjust it and then put it back again. As he went out of the door he said he had only got a little money, but $54,000 would do them a little while. I thought at the time it was simply an extravagant boasting upon his part. It was supposed by the officer I asked that they had got about $5,000.[12]

Just before leaving the coach, wrote Hagerty, the "chief" turned to his captive audience and "repeated a few lines of

Shakespeare, and acted it out as though he knew how to do it."
The preacher didn't know it at the time, but by recording this
seemingly trivial incident he was giving a valuable clue as to the
identity of the train robbers—this robber in particular. It is a
well-known fact that throughout his lifetime Frank James was
an avid reader and quoter of William Shakespeare. What other
Western outlaw would have spouted lines from the Bard of
Avon while robbing a railroad train?

Some historians of Jamesiana have suggested that it might
have been Frank, not Jesse, who selected Gads Hill as the robbery site, doing so in part because of the scene in
Shakespeare's *King Henry IV* in which Sir John Falstaff and
companions robbed a party of travelers on a highway near
Gad's Hill, England.[13] Jesse James was known for his sense of
humor; perhaps brother Frank had one as well.

Hagerty did not tell us which Shakespearean lines the outlaw quoted as he departed the coach that evening, but the passengers would no doubt have found this one from *King Henry
VI* most appropriate:

"Unbidden guests are often welcomest
when they are gone."[14]

CHAPTER 9

"Dish Out, or Be Shot!"

I was in the sleeping car at the time of the robbery; the porter locked the doors and refused to admit the gang; they kicked against the doors as though they intended to break them in.
—News agent Alfred Butler, *St. Louis Times,* February 2, 1874

When news agent Alfred Butler boarded the Little Rock Express in St. Louis that morning, he no doubt presumed it would be just another humdrum day of selling candy, tobacco, and reading material to bored passengers. Never in his wildest dreams would he have imagined that a bizarre event would occur on this run that would cause his name and remarks to later appear in the very newspapers he was peddling.

At the time the train rolled into Gads Hill, Butler, porter James Johnson, and Pullman conductor O. S. Newell were attending passengers in the sleeping car. Upon realizing that a robbery was in progress, Johnson quickly locked the doors. His action, though, did little to discourage the masked trio. When they approached the car and found themselves locked out, they began kicking the door forcefully in an effort to break it open. This greatly alarmed the passengers, and some of them pleaded with Johnson to let the outlaws in. Reluctantly, Johnson unlocked the door. As the three entered, one of them pointed his pistol at Butler's head and shouted, "Dish out, or be shot!" Butler opted to dish out and quickly handed over fifty hard-earned dollars. "One of the gang," he later said, "had a revolver in each hand, and three others in his pocket."[1]

Johnson was next robbed, and he gave such a paltry amount that the bandits suspected him of holding out. One of them shoved a pistol in his ribs and demanded he surrender the rest of his money. The frightened porter swore that two dollars was all he had and, fearing it might go off, begged them not to point the weapon at him. Finally, convinced Johnson was telling the truth, the gunmen left him and proceeded down the aisle. Along the way, they robbed conductor Newell of twenty dollars.

Butler later told a reporter that some of the passengers had hidden their valuables under their seats, "and on this being discovered," he said, "every passenger in the car was made to stand up and turn the cushions so that the seats could be easily searched . . . the plunderers would carefully assort the articles their frightened victims gave them, and return most of them; silver watches they refused to take."

As the robbers approached each male passenger, they asked his name, occupation, and where he was from. The Minnesota travelers, Merriam and Lincoln, being well-to-do Northerners, were by one account forced to hand over about two hundred dollars each.[2] When they learned Lincoln's name, the former rebels could not resist making a few sarcastic comments. The *Ouachita Commercial* reported:

> Against Mr. Lincoln they especially directed a great many not very complimentary or soothing remarks. They thought that "any G— d—— son of a —— that wore that name ought to be shot." But they proceeded to no violence other than language, notwithstanding their in-bred antipathy to Honest Old Abe.[2]

During the confrontation, John Lincoln's hat either fell or was knocked to the floor and was given a swift kick by one of the masked men. In so doing, the outlaw's own hat fell off, giving Lincoln a good view of the shape of his face and head under the mask. Lincoln would later insist that the man who booted his hat that day was Cole Younger.[3]

Sitting near the Minnesotans was another gentleman from Yankee country. His brief conversation with the thieves was later quoted by an unnamed passenger in the car.

"And where are you from?" they asked.

"New England," was the response.[4]

"Ah, ha! You're the chap we're looking for. Shell out here. Shell out!" With a pistol pointing at his breast he handed over his last cent.

The passenger who reported the above episode was questioned next. When he told the robbers that he was a "workingman" from Little Rock, they said they did not wish to disturb him and moved on.

Despite the seriousness of the moment and the threats made against those who were slow to cooperate, the outlaws were generally cheerful and seemed to enjoy themselves immensely. In one instance one of them lifted a hat from the head of a well-dressed passenger and exchanged it with his own battered slouch hat. The passenger, said to have been "slightly intoxicated" at the time, expressed great satisfaction with the trade and "seemed to think everything was lovely." The outlaw's hat later became the possession of a citizen of nearby Piedmont.[5]

The jokes and antics were helpful in easing the passengers' fears and even brought a smile to some. Others, though, were not amused. One man, suspected of being a detective, was taken into a private compartment and forced to disrobe. The outlaws said they were looking for a secret mark that would identify him as a Pinkerton man. The gentleman apparently had no secret mark and aside from being humiliated was not harmed.[6]

Another passenger who had no appreciation for outlaw humor was Mrs. James Morley. She was "terribly frightened," according to Butler, and "cried bitterly" throughout the ordeal. Her husband, Colonel Morley, dutifully stood up and protested the robbery. The words of this important Iron Mountain/Cairo and Fulton executive usually commanded

This steel engraving, which appeared in the Little Rock Arkansas
Gazette, *February 3, 1874, purportedly represented the "captain" of the
Gads Hill band as he had appeared earlier to the stage passengers robbed at
Hot Springs. "He then wore no mask," the newspaper explained. Later,
when suspicious readers commented that the drawing bore a striking resem-
blance to Prince Alexis of Russia, the editor was said to have replied,
"There is nothing remarkable about that," and let the matter drop.
According to the* Gazette, *October 2, 1966, this was the first picture of a
person ever printed in that paper's news columns.*

great respect in railroad matters, but they had no effect here against cocked revolvers. He was promptly ordered "to sit down and shut his head and mind his business." Of course, the colonel felt that he indeed was minding his business, but as conductor Alford later commented, "they didn't seem to agree with him." When Morley asked the robbers to return the passengers' stolen property, they placed a pistol under his nose and ordered him to keep quiet. Their request, so emphasized, seemed reasonable to the colonel and he complied. Morley was fleeced of fifteen dollars. His gold watch was also taken, but returned. Mrs. Morley was not robbed.[7]

The *Little Rock Republican* gave a different and apparently erroneous version of the couple's experience:

> Col. Morley, chief engineer of the Cairo and Fulton railroad, was treated rather considerately. He had given his watch and most of his money to his wife. When the robbers came along he had but ten dollars in his possession. They returned that, saying that he was a d——d pretty chief engineer of a first-class railroad, traveling without a watch and with only a ten-dollar bill.[8]

Mrs. Morley, upon reading the above account, immediately responded by writing the newspaper a scolding letter:

> Little Rock, February 3, 1874.
> Editor Little Rock Republican:
> You have been misinformed in regard to the robbery at Gads Hill in several details—particularly in the assertion that Mr. Morley gave his watch and money to his wife for safe-keeping untrue. The remarks attributed to the robbers in regard to the chief-engineer traveling with only ten dollars and no watch are purely imaginary, as nothing of the kind was said; though it is true that he had very little money with him, which is easily accounted for by giving the same reason that Jack gave for not eating his supper.
>
> Mrs. J. H. Morley.[9]

Sticking its editorial tail between its legs, the *Republican* recanted, stating that its informer was apparently at fault.

The only other female passenger aboard the Pullman car was Mrs. Scott of Pennsylvania. She was carrying a fat purse containing $400 in cash. Until then the outlaw gang had, except for the snatching of three comparatively inexpensive pocket handkerchiefs, obeyed their promise to not rob ladies. Here, however, greed overcame chivalry and they took Mrs. Scott's money, leaving her and her young son only ten cents with which to travel on to Hot Springs.[10]

In other instances the victims were shown more compassion. One passenger, bound for Texas, was robbed of all his money, but when the thieves learned he was in "poor circumstances" and so far from his destination, he was given back fifteen dollars. Another man in a similar situation had five dollars returned.[11]

When the outlaws at last finished their work in the Pullman car, the train robbery was over. There were no more cars, no more passengers, nothing else to rob. All bad things, too, it seems, must come to an end.

Before stepping off the train, one of the trio (some say Jesse James) handed a note to the offensively named passenger, Mr. Lincoln. Surprisingly, it contained the outlaw's own handwritten account of the Gads Hill train robbery, prepared as a press release, newspaper style, complete with a headline and ready for publication. All that was missing was the amount of money taken. The robber had likely composed it at the bonfire during his tedious two-hour wait for the train. Lincoln was instructed that the account be telegraphed to the *St. Louis Dispatch*. That newspaper had misrepresented them on one occasion, the outlaw explained, and this time they wanted to put it in possession of all the facts.[12]

Conductor Alford took charge of the note and later that evening wired its contents word for word to the Iron Mountain Railway headquarters in St. Louis. In the days that followed, a number of newspapers (the *Dispatch* was not among them) would carry the outlaw's account as part of their coverage of the robbery. Printed versions varied slightly, but perhaps the

Old artist's conceptions of the train robbery at Gads Hill.

(From The Border Outlaws, *by James W. Buel, 1881)*

(From The Life, Times, and Treacherous Death of Jesse James, *by Frank J. Triplett, 1882)*

most accurate appeared in the *St. Louis Times,* Sunday morning. It read:

THE MOST DARING ROBBERY ON RECORD

The south bound train on the Iron Mountain railroad was boarded here this evening by five heavily armed men and robbed of _____ dollars. The robbers arrived at the station a few minutes before the arrival of the train and arrested the agent and put him under a guard and then threw the train on the switch. The robbers were all large men, none of them under six feet tall. They were all masked and started in a southerly direction after they had robbed the express. They were all mounted on fine blooded horses. There's a hell of an excitement in this part of the country.

IRA A. MERRILL[13]

Stilson Hutchins, owner of the St. Louis Dispatch. *After holding up the train at Gads Hill, one of the outlaws left behind a self-written press release addressed to Hutchins. The man and his newspaper had misrepresented them on one occasion, the outlaw reportedly stated, and this time they wanted the facts reported correctly. (Author's collection)*

A postscript addressed to Stilson Hutchins, owner of the *St. Louis Dispatch,* read: "You had better send a reporter down here."[14]

While the outlaw's account was accurate for the most part, key elements seem to have been falsely written to mislead—namely, the height description, the direction of retreat, and the "Ira A. Merrill" signature. It is not known who Ira A. Merrill was, or even if he was, but it's a safe bet that he was not one of the Gads Hill train robbers. The editor of the *Little Rock Arkansas Gazette* had his own idea. The outlaw, he decided, had meant to assume the identity of one John A. Murrell, an old-time Southern bandit of decades earlier, and had somehow miswritten the name.[15] In printing the *Gazette* version, the Arkansas editor took it upon himself to change the signature line to read: "John A. Murrell." He also rewrote the direction of retreat to northwest, the direction the robbers actually took.[16]

Having finished their chore of thievery, the three desperadoes stepped from the train and, in Hagerty's words, "walked off as leisurely as any other men towards the house in the rear of us." They left behind a relieved, but angry, trainload of passengers.

PART III

The Retreat

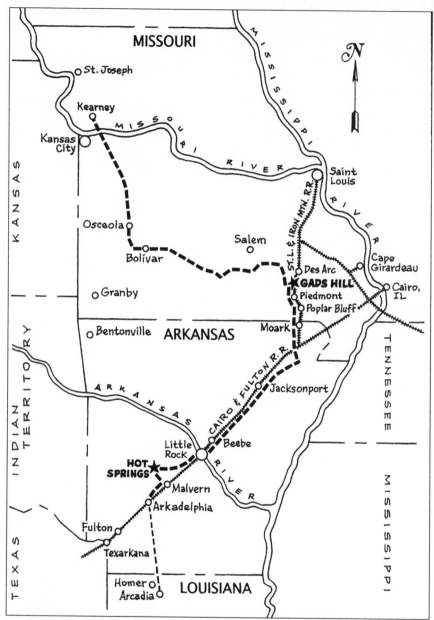

*Approximate travels of the Gads Hill robbers in Arkansas and Missouri.
(The route shown from Arcadia, Louisiana, to Arkadelphia, Arkansas,
assumes they were the same five who robbed the Shreveport-Monroe stage,
January 8.) The outlaws were seen riding out of Arkadelphia, January 13.
Two days later they held up a stagecoach near Hot Springs and then basically followed the Cairo and Fulton rail line to Missouri. After robbing the
train at Gads Hill, they made their way across portions of Reynolds, Dent,
Shannon, Texas, Wright, Laclede, Dallas, and Polk counties, Missouri,
before turning north to their homes. (Map by author)*

CHAPTER 10

Over the Hill and Out of Sight

When we got ready to start, the robbers shook hands with the engineer, Wm. Wetton, and told him whenever he saw a red flag out he ought to stop. They then strolled off to their horses, tied up about a hundred yards distant, and rode out of sight before we got under way.

—Conductor Chauncey Alford, *Bolivar Free Press*,
February 26, 1874

In ensuing years, as the legend of Jesse James continued to grow, most of the Gads Hill victims undoubtedly came to view their misadventure in a somewhat different light. After all, how many people could say they had been robbed by Jesse James? It was at the very least a lifelong conversation piece. Perhaps as time passed, many of these folks developed an attitude similar to that of Prof. J. L. Allen, a Kentucky gentleman who was robbed by Jesse and his gang near Lexington, Missouri, later that same year. Professor Allen remarked to a reporter that "he was exceedingly glad, as he had to be robbed, that it was done by first class artists, by men of national reputation."[1]

Of course, at the time of the Gads Hill train robbery, the passengers—fleeced and unfleeced alike—felt anything but "exceedingly glad." Most were no doubt wishing the scoundrels could be caught and hanged from the nearest tree. One who did not harbor such feelings was Hagerty. True to his profession, the good preacher had a more forgiving attitude. In his letter to the *St Louis Globe* he commented:

> Since the "masked men" were bound to have money, without giving us or the railroad authority any warning, they have my thanks for treating us and the ladies so kindly. I should be glad to meet the boys again, and give them some good advice. In the meantime I will pray for them, that they may be led to forsake their evil course, repent of their sins, and harden their hands with work and honest industry, instead of their hearts with crime and robbery.
>
> If this should fall under the eye of any of them, let them remember that I have no hardness laid up against them, but shall pray for their conversion.[2]

Hagerty's prayers apparently had little effect. Jesse and his gang would continue their "evil course" for another eight years.

The robbery had taken forty minutes to complete. Just how much loot was raked in during that time was never accurately determined. Conductor Alford later told a reporter that the robbers "took in all about $2,500 from the train, four registered packages, one gold watch, five pistols, one ring, and one pin." He added, "Had they made their raid the day before, they would have got about $5,000 or $6,000, which was being shipped by express." Alford was obviously referring to the approximately $5,000 cash that Mr. Staunchfield, superintendent of the Clear Water Lumber Company, had brought down Friday from St. Louis to pay off his company's employees. Staunchfield and the payroll money had been expected on Saturday's train, but as good fortune would have it, he decided to make the trip twenty-four hours earlier.[3]

Express messenger Wilson estimated the train's total loss at $4,000. Another crewman put the amount at about $5,000. Sunday morning the *St. Louis Republican* proclaimed that a whopping $10,000 had been heisted, then Monday "corrected" that figure to $22,000. On the other extreme, Jesse James' widow told the *Kansas City Evening Star* years later that the gang had made only $2,000 at Gads Hill.⁴ At least that's what Jesse told her.

Reports of individual losses often varied as well. Silas Ferry, for instance, was robbed of $7.50, $70.50, $750, or $57, depending on which newspaper one read; John Merriam lost $200, $360, or $50; and news agent Alfred Butler (sometimes unflatteringly referred to as the "train boy") handed over $50, $40, or $11.

Despite the very definite statements of Hagerty and C. H. Henry that several "workingmen" were passed over because they had callous hands, almost every one of the twelve male passengers claimed to have been robbed. Did the press err? It certainly did in many other instances. Or did some of the less-scrupulous passengers make false claims in an attempt to bilk the railroad? Unfortunately, these questions cannot be answered.⁵

Whatever amount was taken, the robbers did not seem pleased. Bill Wilson later told a reporter that he heard one of them say "they would not have bothered the train if they had known there was so little money on board. They thought it being the last of the month the road would be remitting considerable money to various points."

Pleased or not, the brigands were now ready to leave, and conductor Alford was eager to get back on the road. "When I thought they had got about through," he later stated, "I asked them if I might go. They said yes, and I sent a man to shut the northern switch and went myself to shut the southern." While Alford was so engaged, the outlaws released the hostage train crew, shook hands with each, and thanked them for being so kind. They joked with the engineer and told him to always be sure to stop whenever he saw a red flag. Wetton assured them he always did.

After lighting the headlamp on his engine, Wetton climbed aboard and prepared to run the train back onto the main track. Suddenly, one of the outlaws rushed forward and shouted, "Stop!" Quickly stepping in front of the steaming locomotive, he stooped and retrieved his overcoat from the tracks where he had left it prior to the train's arrival. With coat in hand, and perhaps blushing just a bit under the mask, he waved the engineer on.[6] The robbers then made for the clump of oak saplings where their horses were tethered. (One of those saplings eventually grew into a large tree and survived well into the mid-twentieth century, known in local legend as "the tree where Jesse James tied his horse.")[7]

Conductor Alford had considerable difficulty shutting the south switch. "They had bent the rod so that I had to get a board and straighten it," he said. "This took me some time, and in the meanwhile they made off."

Before departing, the robbers relieved the village of three fine saddle horses—spare mounts they knew would be needed during the hard night ride that lay ahead. According to the *St. Louis Democrat,* they still had with them the stagecoach horse they had stolen two weeks earlier in Arkansas.[8] Within a few minutes the bandits were over the hill and out of sight. No one was unhappy to see them go.

It was dark by then, or nearly so, the sun having set at 5:21 P.M. Although this night was the eve of a full moon, that heavenly orb the outlaws had counted on to brighten their way was now shrouded by a cloudy sky.[9] The air was cold and damp and already there were flurries of snow.

Guided by map and compass, the train robbers set an overland course northwest into the rugged Ozark hills, country more suited to Missouri mules than to horses. Forcing their long-legged roadsters across this mountainous terrain, the robbers moved like shadows in the night; the only sounds heard were the labored breathing of their animals and the rustle underfoot as they stumbled noisily through the dark and seemingly unending forest of oak and pine. Ahead lay a difficult journey, one that would take them across the breadth of Missouri. To Frank James and his traveling companions, the "good country" must have seemed forever away.

Sometime before 6:00 P.M., the express finally pulled out of Gads Hill. The smoke cleared and the rumble and rattle gradually faded as the train distanced itself southward. The village was again quiet.

Womenfolk returned to their homes, lit coal-oil lamps, and rekindled stove fires. Children, still mystified by what had just happened, clung apprehensively to their mothers' aprons. Outside, the men doused the smoldering bonfire and huddled awhile to discuss the robbery and to decide what should be done about it come sunup.

At last Mr. Farris and Billy bade a weary "good night," bundled themselves against the cold night air, and turned their horses westerly toward Reynolds County. Tom Fitz set out for Des Arc, and the village men went inside their houses to get warm. It had been a most trying evening for all.

Meanwhile, as the express continued its journey, the outside world had yet to hear of its harrowing experience with highwaymen. That was about to change. At the next stop, Piedmont, conductor Alford would set the telegraph wires a-humming with news of Missouri's first train robbery—news that would be printed in towns and cities throughout the nation and be forever a part of the history and legend of Jesse James.

CHAPTER 11

"A Hell of an Excitement"

There is great excitement over the affair at Gads Hill. . . . A number of our citizens are preparing to start to scour the country in search of the robbers. Not less than fifty mounted men will go.
—*St. Louis Republican*, February 1, 1874 (special dispatch from Piedmont, Missouri)

At Piedmont, seven miles down the line, it was more or less a typical Saturday evening in an Ozark lumber town. Most folks had just finished supper. The dishes were washed, the livestock was fed, and families were relaxing by the fire in the comfort of their respective parlors. Some had already gone to bed. Others, like the transient sawmill workers who were prone to spend their hard-earned end-of-the-month wages on liquor, gambling, and saloon girls, were just beginning to whoop it up in local dramshops.

Meanwhile, down at the railroad depot things were a bit more serious. The station agent and his crew were anxiously awaiting arrival of the express train out of St. Louis, and this evening it was running late—very late. It had obviously met with some major difficulty, they concluded. But what? There were no telegrams—no word of any kind. More than once a station worker would step out into the crisp night air to squint northward and listen. Each time he would be greeted only by silent darkness and swirling flurries of snow.

Minutes ticked by. The waiting and uneasiness continued. Then, at last, from far up the track came that familiar shrill whistle. The Little Rock Express was coming in!

Bill Wetton, running his engine at full throttle, breathed a heavy sigh of relief when he saw the friendly lights of Piedmont filtering through the trees ahead. Piedmont was equally relieved when it saw Bill. As the station men stepped out to greet the train, Wetton ordered "down brakes" and moments later, with bell clanging and boiler hissing steam, the locomotive and its small procession of cars came to a screeching halt in front of the depot. The first person off was conductor Alford. In his hand was the outlaw-written press release. Its prophetic last line was about to be realized; there would indeed be "a hell of an excitement in this part of the country."

As the small crowd gathered round, Alford made a most incredible announcement. His train had just been boarded and robbed back at Gads Hill! Masked gunmen had gone through the express safe and mailbags and had made paupers of most of the passengers and crew! Alford's story hit his listeners like a Civil War cannon ball. Some wanted to hear more. Others sprinted off to tell the town. Word of the robbery spread quickly, and in no time at all the Piedmont train yard was swarming with excited villagers eager to hear the details.

After briefly telling his story, Alford made haste to the telegraph office, where he wired news of the robbery to his employers at the Iron Mountain Railway headquarters in St. Louis. The operator there notified the local press, which in turn telegraphed newspapers in other cities. Wires were also sent to railroad stations up and down the line and to the county sheriff's office in Greenville. It was a busy night for Western Union.

As soon as the conductor completed his duties, he signaled engineer Wetton, and the train moved on. Mr. Henry got off at the next stop, Clear Water; he had more business to conduct in St. Louis and would catch the northbound back to the city the following morning. Hagerty debarked another thirty-five miles down the road, at Poplar Bluff, where he was met by Christian friends and whisked away to a late supper and warm bed.[1]

From Poplar Bluff the Little Rock Express and its plundered passengers proceeded south toward the flat country of northeastern Arkansas and arrived at the state line about 9:30 that evening. At Moark, Alford and his fellow trainmen were replaced by a fresh crew. They would spend the night there, as scheduled, and resume their duties the next day on the train back to St. Louis.

The Express, with its new crew, then followed the Cairo and Fulton line on into central Arkansas. In the early morning hours it crossed the Arkansas River via the recently completed Baring Cross Bridge and, moments later, pulled into the Little Rock station. News reporters were on hand to interview the passengers.

Sunday dawned in Southeast Missouri, and citizens awoke to a light blanket of new-fallen snow. The weather, cold as it was, did not chill the intense fervor created by events of the previous evening. While emotions obviously ran higher in the vicinity of Gads Hill, they were strongly felt elsewhere as well. People had gathered at favorite meeting places all along the Iron Mountain line, and the topic of every conversation was the train robbery. It was hard to believe that a small band of marauders—they knew not who—had been so brash as to hold up a railroad train in their state. It had never been done before in Missouri—not in peacetime anyway. If one word could have described how most Missourians viewed the bold event, the *St. Louis Republican* must surely have found it. Its lead headline that morning read simply: "AUDACIOUS."

In St. Louis, the morning train was pulling out of Plum Street Station just as its ill-fated Iron Mountain cousin had done twenty-four hours earlier. This time, however, there was one noticeable difference; the crewmen on this particular run were openly packing revolvers and shotguns. Similar precautions were being taken on the northbound leaving Little Rock for St. Louis. The railroad company in Arkansas had hired four extra firemen and engineers to ride shotgun on the locomotive. If a second attack were to occur, these trainmen apparently figured to make a fight of it.

THE RAILROAD ROBBERY

More Explicit Account of the Dare-Devil Operation.

The Robbers Recognized as the Hot Springs Plunderers.

A Merchant of Gad's Hill Also Gone Through.

The National Uniform Used As a Travelling Disguise.

Extreme Nicety of Distinction on Part of the Villains.

Ladies and Workingmen Exempt---Plug-Hats in Demand.

On the Lookout for Pinkerton's Detectives

[Special Dispatch to the Republican.]
PIEDMONT, Mo., Feb. 1.—Nothing has, as yet, been heard of the desperadoes who robbed the Little Rock express last evening.

Early this morning about twenty-five horsemen, well armed, started from Gad's Hill in pursuit. They were strongly reinforced on their route. They took a northwesterly course, the direction in which the robbers fled, and were in hopes of striking their trail.

A slight snow-storm last night will materially assist them. Nothing, however, has been heard from the pursuers up to the present time.

It appears from information received here that the robbers committed some depredations at Hot Springs, Arks., from which place they started on Tuesday last. They took dinner at Mill Spring, six miles south of this place, on Friday last, and passed through this town on horseback. During the afternoon they wore federal overcoats, and all carried muskets.

On Friday night they stopped at the Widow Gilbreath's, about three miles north of this place. Upon taking off their overcoats it was seen that each man was armed with two revolvers.

A portion of an article that appeared on the front page of the St. Louis Republican, *Monday morning, February 2, 1874. It typified the accounts printed in newspapers soon after the train was robbed.*

In the Carondelet community in south St. Louis, railroad men had collected on Main Street and at the depot and round-house to exchange thoughts on the robbery. Thoughts were not all they were exchanging. "Trading and speculation in revolvers and other weapons is lively," wrote a visiting reporter, "every fire-man and brakeman being desirous of equipping himself with a brace of six-shooters." There was also a rush to buy newspapers. The demand was "greater than could be supplied," it was noted.

Forty miles to the south, in De Soto, the scene was much the same. Railroad men and townsfolk were "thoroughly aroused," observed the *St. Louis Times,* "and . . . proposed to organize a company for the purpose of hunting down the desperadoes." It was generally believed in De Soto that the robbers were the same band who had held up the stagecoach near Hot Springs two weeks earlier, and that local badman Sam Hildebrand was their leader.[2]

In Gads Hill and neighboring villages, there was far more than just talk. A dispatch sent Saturday night from Piedmont to the *St. Louis Republican* had boasted that a number of local citi-zens ("not less than fifty") were preparing to set out in search of the thieves. Now, as morning broke, the citizens were making every effort to carry out that promise. Men of all ages, mounted on horses and mules, had armed themselves with muzzle-load-ing squirrel rifles, shotguns, pistols—whatever they had in their private arsenals—and were eagerly awaiting the arrival of Sheriff Benjamin Holmes and his order to set out on the manhunt. The fifty-three-year-old former Confederate colonel was en route from Greenville,[3] a distance of about twenty-two miles. Despite the snowfall, the volunteers felt confident that under Colonel Holmes' capable leadership they could track the rascals down.

As the prospective posse assembled, three adventurous young men, armed and ready for action, rode down from Des Arc. Too impatient to wait for the sheriff and perhaps dreaming of fame and reward money, they decided to strike out through the woods on their own. Fortunately, the night's snow, much of which had caught in tree branches, had not been heavy, and tracking the robbers offered no serious problems. After several hours of hard riding, however, the boys returned, saying they had followed the trail for six miles but lost it at a ford on Black River.[4]

Eventually, Sheriff Holmes arrived and organized the posse, and the official search got under way. The actual number of horsemen who started from Gads Hill proved to be only half the proposed fifty, but others did join in as the chase progressed. Among those late joiners were fifteen of Mr. Farris's neighbors in Reynolds County, "all game men and well-armed."[5] The efforts of Holmes' posse, though, would prove as futile as those of the young Des Arc trio. Even a hundred men armed with a dozen Gatling guns could not have captured the James-Younger train robbers that day. Their superior horses and many hours' head start made overtaking them virtually impossible.

As the pursuers followed the outlaw trail across the Ozarks, crowds continued to gather at railroad stations. Many had come just to get in on the excitement; others were there to hear the latest news and perhaps catch a glimpse of conductor Alford and his now-famous Gads Hill crew as their train passed through on its way back to St. Louis.

At 3:30 P.M. the train arrived in De Soto, and the crewmen were immediately mobbed by well-wishers who wanted to shake their hands and congratulate them at having survived the encounter. In the crowd was Alford's wife, Elizabeth, who had journeyed down from the couple's south St. Louis home to meet his train. After assuring her he was all right, the conductor made a statement to the press. News agent Al Butler and passenger Henry also made statements. When the interviews were over, Alford signaled his engineer, and the northbound resumed its trip to St. Louis.

Soon after sundown the train pulled into Plum Street Station, and the weary crewmen parted company. Chauncey and Elizabeth Alford[6] headed home to Carondelet; the others went to their respective places of abode. It was good to be home. It was good to be alive.

For the conductor and his crew, the adventure was over. For Sheriff Holmes and his Wayne County posse, it had only just begun.

CHAPTER 12

On the Trail of Jesse James

St. Louis, Feb. 13—Gov. Woodson, of this State, will issue a proclamation tomorrow, offering a reward of $2,000 apiece, dead or alive, for the men who robbed the passenger express and mail train on the Iron Mountain Railroad at Gads Hill, Jan. 31. In addition to this it is understood the Governor of Arkansas has offered $2,500, and the Post Office Department $5,000, making an aggregate of $17,500.[1]

—*New York Times,* February 14, 1874

The Wayne County posse was now in full pursuit of the train bandits, and the railroad and express companies had engaged the Pinkerton National Detective Agency to join the chase. The object of the manhunt, so speculated the *St. Louis Dispatch,* was a "famous quintette of bank robbers" who hailed mostly from northwestern Missouri. "Arthur McCoy, Jesse and Frank James, and Cole and Budd Younger are the men in question," it stated, "and are without doubt the most daring band of robbers the country ever contained."[2]

Most readers of the *Dispatch* probably accepted the accusations at face value, but a few did not. For one thing, Cole Younger had no relative named Budd; it was, in fact, Cole himself who was known as "Bud" during the war. As for Cole, he was in Louisiana when the train was robbed—at least that's how he and his friends remembered it. And Arthur McCoy had an even better alibi; one of his pals claimed he was dead. (The guilt or innocence of these and other suspects will be examined more extensively in a later chapter.)

Among those who believed—or wanted to believe—that the James brothers were innocent of the crime was their good friend and defender, John Newman Edwards, editor of the *Dispatch*. Edwards was away in Jefferson City when the article appeared, and, upon reading in his own newspaper that the boys were being accused of train robbery, he became furious. Calling the account stupid and untrue, he immediately sent a scathing telegram to his city editor, Walter B. Stevens, ordering that nothing more be printed about the matter.[3] Circumstantial evidence and popular opinion, however, would continue to point to the Jameses and Youngers as the Gads Hill bandits.

John Newman Edwards, well-known newspaper man and defender of the James and Younger brothers. (Author's collection)

While debate continued over who the guilty party might have been, the robbers were leading their pursuers on a merry chase across the Ozark Mountains. Riding hard over hill and hollow, they followed roadways, forded creeks and rivers, and trekked through fields and forest. Along the way they camped beside streams, ate and slept at farmhouses, and bought or stole horses as needed. Soon, newspapers were giving sketchy accounts of their activities and pinpointing many of the places where they stopped or passed. Aided by these old news accounts, contemporary maps, a story or two handed down by old-timers, and a wee bit of common logic, we will attempt to retrace that ancient trail.

From Gads Hill the James-Younger gang fled northwest toward Reynolds County, and after a few miles of hard riding, they supposedly stopped for supper at the home of a Civil War widow. According to an undated *Ozark Graphic* newspaper clipping, the story was told in the mid-1950s by an elderly Wayne County resident who was a boy at the time of the train robbery. The old man claimed he had heard the widow herself tell the story to his mother and other neighborhood women at a quilting party just days after the incident occurred.

On "the night of the snow" (January 31, 1874), he said, the woman had just blown out the lamp and crawled into bed when her dogs began barking. Moments later she heard horses approach and then a knock at her door. When she asked who was there, a stranger's voice answered. Assuring her that he and his friends meant no harm, the man said they were hungry travelers and, if she would please cook supper for them, they would eat and be on their way. With some apprehension she opened the door. As the stranger entered, he politely removed his hat. His coat was lightly powdered with snow, she recalled, and bulged as if concealing weapons. Somewhat comforted by his gentle demeanor, the widow went to work frying up some bacon, eggs, and cornbread. She also brought out a jar of honey, and one of the men asked for butter, which she kept on her porch during cold weather.

The men ate in shifts, it was told. While one was enjoying his meal, others were busy outside splitting wood and stacking it on the porch. Armloads were also brought in and placed beside the cooking and heating stoves. As soon as one man finished eating, he would pick up the axe and take his turn at the wood pile; then another hungry man would come and sit at the table. Before the evening was over, her visitors were well fed, and the woman had a more than adequate supply of firewood.

It was late when the men finally left, the old storyteller said. As they walked out the door, one of them thanked the widow and handed her a fistful of coins. Moments later they were back on their horses and riding off into the darkness. The woman told her friends at the quilting party that she didn't sleep a wink the rest of the night.[4]

Tales of Jesse's generosity to the poor during his flight from Gads Hill have been told and retold for generations, and no small few involve women who had lost their husbands. It seems this "noble" outlaw was always being kind to poor widows, but that's not surprising. After all, because of Jesse James and his gang, there were more poor widows to be kind to.

The train robbers continued their flight and apparently crossed Black River at the ford where the three Des Arc boys said they lost the trail. An 1874 map of Reynolds County indicates such a river crossing on the old Lesterville road, almost exactly six miles northwest of Gads Hill.[5] From there, it is believed, the outlaws took the road north along the river, in the direction of Lesterville. In his later years, Billy Farris (the boy who met his father's train) recalled that the posse came upon a stake in the road with a note attached. It allegedly read: "If you want to see us, we will be camped on upper Sinking Creek. Jesse James." Whether the posse found such a note or not, some claim the outlaws did camp briefly on upper Sinking Creek.[6]

Holmes' posse followed the trail farther into Reynolds County and, some sixteen miles north and west of Gads Hill, reached the three forks of Black River. Near the mouth of East Fork the main channel bends sharply westward and joins Middle Fork near Lesterville. Somewhere on the middle fork of Black River, about eighteen miles into the chase, the pursuers came upon a spent horse the robbers had left behind.

The *Salem Success* reported that it was one of the three stolen at Gads Hill and belonged to a member of the posse.[7] (According to old Billy Farris, one of the stolen horses was the property of posse member Frank Carter. Frank didn't recover his horse, said Billy, but when an outlaw's jaded animal was found abandoned on the trail, Frank kept it as his own.)

The train robbers were now traveling in a westerly direction along Black River's west fork. Rapid passage over this rugged terrain continued to take its toll on their stock and even the best horses eventually played out. As they did, it became necessary to buy or "borrow" fresh ones. Reports suggest that Jesse and his men borrowed far more than they bought.

One of their first "horse trades" seems to have been made with a Reynolds County farmer named James Sutterfield, who lived with his wife, Elizabeth, and children near the confluence of West Fork and Tom's Creek. This story was first told to me in 1988 by a well-respected resident of the county, eighty-six-year-old Amel Martin. Amel's father, he said, was a close friend and neighbor of "Uncle Jimmy" Sutterfield, and Amel had grown up with the story. He recalled hearing it this way:

A night or two after the train robbery, a group of heavily armed men rode up to the Sutterfield home and tied their horses at the barn across the road. They called Jimmy outside and told him they wanted to buy a horse. One of theirs was completely exhausted and had to be replaced. The strangers said they were willing to pay a fair price but made it clear that should Jimmy refuse to sell, they would take the horse anyway. Having heard it explained in those terms, Jimmy agreed to a deal.

Elizabeth fixed supper for the men, said Amel, and after the meal they and Jimmy went to the barn, where the transaction was completed. As soon as the purchaser transferred his saddle to the fresh mount, he turned, drew a pistol, and, for reasons known only to himself, shot the jaded horse in the head. The party then mounted and rode away.

The next morning when Jimmy went out to dispose of the "dead" animal, he was shocked to find it still very much alive and standing in the barnyard. In time the injured horse was

James and Elizabeth Sutterfield with seven of their thirteen children (ca. 1895) in front of the old log house where, two decades earlier, Jesse James and his men stopped and bought a horse. (Courtesy of Floyd Sutterfield)

nursed back to health, and it survived for many years on the Sutterfield farm, locally famous as having once been "owned by Jesse James."[8]

The Sutterfield story was not mentioned in contemporary newspapers, per se, but the *Salem Success* may have been referring to the incident when it briefly stated: "In one instance [the outlaws] paid $130 for a horse and shot one they were riding, substituting the fresh one."[9] Unfortunately, the paper didn't give the seller's name, nor where the transaction took place.

The five horsemen evidently departed West Fork at the Sutterfield farm and followed Tom's Creek southwest, passing just north of present-day Bunker, Missouri. Thirteen miles after entering Dent County they reached Gladden Valley and

James ("Uncle Jimmy") Sutterfield in later years. (Courtesy of Floyd Sutterfield)

turned south. A short time later they were seen riding past the farm of an L. F. Snelson, who lived with his family on Gladden Creek, about twelve miles south of Salem. According to the Salem newspaper, eleven men were then in pursuit.

Gladden Creek flows into Current River in northwestern Shannon County, sixty miles west and slightly north of Gads Hill. The outlaws reached that area on the evening of Tuesday, February 3, and stopped at the home of a widow named Cook. Mrs. Cook's cabin stood about a mile upriver from the now-extinct post-office settlement of Carpenterville[10] and about one-half mile above the mouth of Gladden Creek, site of present-day Akers. The Salem newspaper reported:

> Last week we published an account of a daring train robbery at Gads Hill, on the Iron Mountain railroad, since which time it is believed the parties committing the robbery have been seen in

[Dent County]. On Tuesday night . . . five men put up at the residence of Widow Cook, on Current River [in Shannon County], eighteen miles south of Salem. They were well armed, and mounted, and one of their number was placed on guard through the night. They had in their possession a map and compass by which they travelled, and consulted the same at Mrs. Cook's. Accompanying the party was a loose horse. . . . The country over which they passed is extremely rough and difficult of passage, whereas a detour of a few miles would have given them good roads all the way.[11]

The *St. Louis Republican* also reported the outlaws' visit but claimed they stayed with Mrs. Cook Sunday night rather than Tuesday. (Based on their later activities, this appears to have been an error.) Mrs. Cook's descriptions of the men were similar to those given by conductor Alford, and she agreed with Mr. Farris by stating that two of them were "apparently brothers, being very much alike in form and face."

The visitors arose early, paid their bill, and left at about 4:00 A.M. The *Republican* told of their departure:

They had a map and compass to direct their route, avoiding roads and keeping to the hills as much as possible. They were heavily armed, each having three revolvers. At Widow Cook's they recapped their arms and in travelling went two abreast about one hundred yards apart, the odd man leading the horse in the rear.[12]

Two miles up Current River from Mrs. Cook lived another widow lady, Elizabeth Hodges Howell, known in later life as "Aunt Betsy." Her log cabin stood across the river on a wooded bluff about one-half mile below Welch Spring, where Thomas Welch then owned and operated a large grist mill.[13] The *Salem Success* reported that the Gads Hill outlaws crossed Current River "near the Welch mill" (probably at Howell's Ford, the crossing nearest the mill). That would have put them practically in Betsy's front yard, a fact that makes the following story more plausible.

It is well known and often told in northwestern Shannon County that one day a band of horsemen stopped at the Howell cabin and asked Betsy if she would cook for them. Although she had few groceries on hand, she killed a couple of chickens and was able to prepare a satisfying meal. The strangers numbered four, it is said, and ate in twos. Two ate while two stood guard outside. When all four had eaten, they mounted their horses and rode away. Before leaving, one of them supposedly told Betsy that if anyone came asking for the James or Younger brothers, he and his party would be camped at the big spring in Dooley Hollow. As she was clearing the table, so goes the story, she found a twenty-dollar gold piece under each plate.[14]

If it is true that Betsy Howell did indeed feed the Gads Hill outlaws, the story may have been altered over time. We know, of course, that there were five train robbers, not four. And twenty dollars a plate? Even Robin Hood would have winced at that large amount. One might also wonder why they would have stopped again so soon after leaving Widow Cook's home. Quite possibly they rode off that morning without eating breakfast and, upon seeing a light in Mrs. Howell's window, forded the river and asked to be fed. We'll never know.

There is another story presumably related to the Howell visit. Sometime after Jesse and his men left the neighborhood, two boys, Jefferson Lewis and a lad named Moffit, were tramping through the woods and happened upon a fine-looking pistol lying in the leaves. It had apparently been dislodged from its owner's holster by a grapevine or heavy brush. They picked up the weapon, admired it, and fired it once or twice. After a short while the outlaws came riding back. Jesse asked if they had found a pistol. Yes, Lewis said, and handed it over. Jesse supposedly gave the boys a small reward for their honesty.

It is also told that the James boys hid some money near Welch Cave, but of course that same legend has been similarly attached at one time or another to nearly every cave in Missouri.[15]

Whether any of these old stories are fact, fiction, or a little of both is anybody's guess. What we do know is that contemporary news accounts state that in the predawn hours of February 4, 1874, the Gads Hill train robbers crossed Current River near the grist mill at Welch Spring and proceeded west toward Big Creek in Texas County. That river crossing, as previously stated, likely took place via the ford at Howell's cabin. (Now owned by the National Park Service, who bought the property in 1969 from Earl and Ida Mae Maggard, the historic old Howell cabin has recently been restored as nearly as possible to its original appearance. It is known today as the Maggard cabin.)[16]

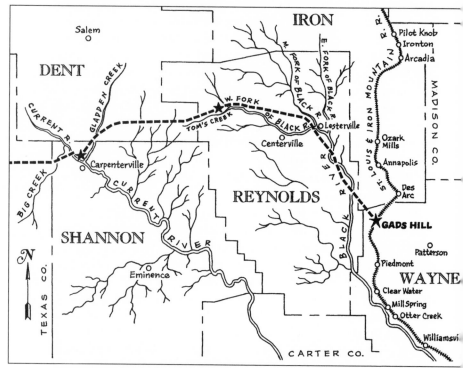

Approximate travels of the Gads Hill robbers in Reynolds, Dent, and Shannon counties, Missouri. After robbing the train at Gads Hill, the James-Younger gang rode northwest and, by way of the Lesterville road, traveled to the three forks of Black River. They reportedly left a spent horse on Middle Fork and later bought a horse from a farmer at the confluence of West Fork and Tom's Creek. From there they rode to Gladden Valley, turned south to Current River, and stopped for the night at Widow Cook's near Carpenterville. The next morning, about two miles upstream, they crossed the river and supposedly stopped for breakfast at Widow Howell's cabin before heading west into Texas County. (Map by author)

It is believed that during their retreat through Shannon County, the Gads Hill outlaws crossed Current River at this ford one-half mile below Welch Spring. Across the river and uphill to the left (out of view) stands the historic Howell cabin, where, according to family legend, the robbers stopped for a meal.

The recently restored Howell cabin. Now owned by the National Park Service, it is known today as the Maggard cabin, after its last occupants.

As Jesse and his comrades continued to outdistance the posse, rumors began circulating that the gang had split up and fled back into Arkansas. Another, also untrue, was that the leader had been captured. These stories were no doubt sparked by incidents reported in Little Rock newspapers.

Train passengers on the Cairo and Fulton were informed at O'Kean Station in northeastern Arkansas that "two of the robbers were seen crossing Beaver Creek, about 3 o'clock Wednesday afternoon [February 4], going south," the *Little Rock Republican* stated. "Their horses looked tired and jaded and were covered with mud."[17] These men, whoever they might have been, were apparently not pursued.

In another instance (reported in the *Little Rock Arkansas Gazette*), a mud-splattered horseman riding near Coldwell, Arkansas, was captured at shotgun-point by two reward-seeking citizens and taken to Searcy for questioning. The men felt certain they had brought in the notorious bandit Arthur McCoy and would be hailed as heroes. Such was not the case, however. The gentleman was promptly released when his red-faced captors learned they had in fact nabbed General Edgarton, an agent of the United States Post Office Department who was in the neighborhood investigating mail fraud.[18]

There were other false sightings as well, in both Arkansas and Missouri. Usually the men in question were two or three in number, muddy, well mounted, and conspicuously avoiding main roads. It seemed that nearly every stranger riding a horse or mule within a hundred-mile radius of Gads Hill was now being viewed with suspicion.

Amid all this confusion, though, the real train robbers—all five—were still galloping high and dry across the Ozark wilderness of Southeast Missouri.

CHAPTER 13

Homeward to the "Good Country"

The robbers of the railroad train at Gads Hill have been traced through Reynolds, Shannon, Dent, Texas, Wright, Laclede, Dallas and Polk counties. . . . As the head-quarters of these men is known to be in St. Clair county, it is a natural supposition to believe that they were making for that destination.

—*Bolivar Free Press,* February 19, 1874

By now these hard-riding highwaymen were the talk of the state. Although most of the talk was unfavorable, there were many who expressed a certain admiration. Comparisons to Robin Hood and other such outlaw heroes were inevitable. The train bandits had, after all, concentrated most of their efforts on the "plug hat gentlemen" at Gads Hill and refused to rob "workingmen." They had laughed and joked during the robbery, were courteous to women and children, and, not unlike the merry men of old, had returned cash and valuables to some of their less fortunate victims. Now, as they retreated across Missouri with pocketfuls of train loot, the outlaws seemed to be generously doling out money to poor widows and farmers. These actions did not go unnoticed by the press. "All along the route," stated one St. Louis newspaper, "they are reported to have conducted themselves as gentlemen, paying for everything they got."[1] Another similarly noted: "They were very extravagant of money, paying all their bills lavishly as they go."[2] Some people were beginning to wonder if the train robbers were really such bad men after all.

As the James and Younger brothers performed these minor acts of chivalry, they were unwittingly creating a legend that would endure even into the next millennium. Among the old stories to survive is the well-known tale of Jesse James, the widow, and the greedy banker. Although historians generally regard it as myth, there are some who believe that the incident actually occurred. When or where, no one knows; but some say it took place during the gang's retreat from Gads Hill. There are several versions of the story. The one that follows is typical:

Jesse James and his men, flush with cash from a recent robbery, were riding through the Missouri Ozarks when they stopped for food at the home of a young widow. As they ate their meal, she tearfully told them that the mortgage on her farm was due, and she had no money to pay it. The banker, she said, was coming that very afternoon to put her and her two small children out in the cold. After listening sympathetically to the woman's story, Jesse kindly forked over the amount she needed. "When you pay the man," Jesse instructed, "be sure you make him burn the mortgage." She promised she would, and the outlaws rode off.

A short time later, the arrogant banker, fully expecting to take possession of the farm, drove up and demanded the money. Much to his surprise and disappointment, the widow paid him. He wrote her a receipt and burned the mortgage; then, with his wallet bulging with cash, he climbed into his buggy and headed back toward town. He had not gone far, however, when out of the brush stepped Jesse James brandishing a cocked revolver. In true Robin Hood fashion, Jesse took back the money and sent the greedy banker on his not-so-merry way.

While such stories did a lot toward promoting the Jesse James legend, newspapermen did their share as well. In Arkansas, a starry-eyed journalist wrote that incidents connected with Hot Springs and Gads Hill reminded him "of the days when Dick Turpin, Claude Duval, Sixteen-String Jack and others of that type, played the roles of robber-knights and high-toned chivalrous thieves on Hounslow heath and the highways of the British isles." He continued, "In modern times, the boldness, recklessness and perfect sang froid of these rascals cannot, in our memory find a parallel. They are vulgar fellows, to be sure, as their blasphemy and general language betray, but their recklessness, and the easy manner in which they go about and transact their 'little jobs,' casts something like a halo of romance around them."[3]

Newspapers in eastern cities voiced similar views. A *Boston Post* journalist wrote: "Not even Claude Duval dancing a minuet with the Duchess and returning her jewels represented any better courtesy of the road than did these five who avoided inflicting unnecessary inconvenience upon their victims." But he hastened to add: "Such refinement . . . ought to have weight with the public, and if the scoundrels can be caught it is to be hoped that they will be consigned to the Missouri Penitentiary with that same promptness and politeness that they employed in their own business."[4]

The law, of course, shared the latter view and, unfortunately for Jesse James and his gang, in much harsher terms.

At that particular point in time, the train robbers were probably not all that concerned with their public image. They just wanted to get home. After departing Betsy Howell's cabin on Current River, they proceeded west across Razor Hollow. A couple or so miles of hard riding later, they forded Big Creek and continued the same course into Texas County. That afternoon, February 4, five men answering their description rode past the home of a Mr. Payne on Big Piney River. They were then reportedly traveling in the direction of Hartville.[5]

By nightfall, still on the Big Piney and about two miles northwest of Houston, Missouri, the outlaws reached the Lebanon road. They stopped there at the home of Dexter and Laura Mason, a couple in their early sixties. At the time, Dexter Mason, soon to be elected state representative of Texas

County, was away on political business in Jefferson City. His wife was home alone. Although no doubt a bit uncomfortable with the situation, she agreed to feed the travelers and put them up for the night.

What Laura Mason and her visitors talked about during their stay is not known, but it is unlikely that the conversation included Gads Hill. The uneasy hostess had heard about the train robbery and was quite certain she was entertaining the very rascals who had done the deed. Still, the gun-toting quintet was well mannered and gave her no reason to be afraid. The next morning after paying their bill, Jesse and his friends mounted up and set off in the direction of Lebanon.

Later that day three farmers stopped at the house and told Mrs. Mason they were searching for a band of thieves who had stolen their horses. She told them about her house guests and pointed in the direction they had traveled. The men left, and Mrs. Mason, much excited over her big adventure, quickly dashed off a letter to her husband in Jefferson City. In turn, Dexter telegraphed the *St. Louis Republican,* which printed the following:

> The Hon. Mr. Mason of Texas county has just received a letter from his wife, giving an account of her experience with the "Men of Gads Hill." On last Wednesday night five men, all armed to the teeth, made their appearance at his residence, and asked shelter for the night. They were all well-dressed and behaved very genteely. They were well-mounted, and led an extra horse. The residence of the Hon. Mr. Mason is on the Big Piney, in Texas county. The five armed men remained during the night. While at the house they conducted themselves very properly, and seemed to be gentlemen in manner and bearing. Thursday morning the five armed men rode away taking the road leading toward Lebanon, in a northwest direction. The indications are that instead of making their way through the southwest wilds to the Indian Territory, the men of Gads Hill are making their way toward the Iowa or Kansas border. It is possible that other trains may be stopped and plundered by these brigands. The day the five armed men left the residence of Mr.

Mason, a party of three men passed in pursuit of a party of horse thieves who had taken their horses. There is no doubt in the mind of Mr. Mason that the five men who remained at his house last Wednesday night are the bandits of Gads Hill.[6]

From the Mason home the "bandits of Gads Hill" appear to have continued on the Lebanon road until they reached a crossroad at the tiny settlement of Good Hope,[7] some six miles distant. Turning left, they struck out in the direction of Wright County.

Sometime Thursday, the same day Jesse and his gang left Laura Mason, eleven horsemen rode up to Widow Cook's

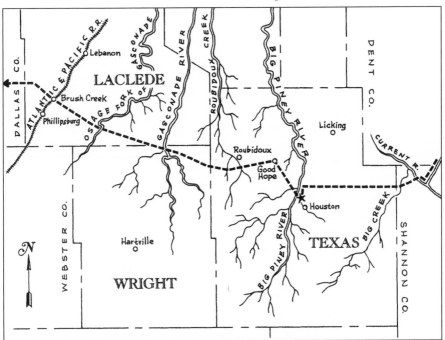

Approximate travels of the Gads Hill robbers in Texas, Wright, and Laclede counties, Missouri. The fleeing train robbers crossed Big Creek and rode westward across Texas County. They stayed at the Mason home on Big Piney River and the next morning took the Lebanon road northwest. Turning west again (probably at Good Hope) the horsemen passed through a portion of Wright County, rode into Laclede County, and crossed the Atlantic and Pacific railroad at Brush Creek. From there they traveled to Bolivar in Polk County and, soon after, apparently turned north to their homes in St. Clair and Clay counties. (Map by author)

home back in Shannon County. They explained that they were a sheriff's posse on the trail of five desperadoes and asked the widow if she had seen anyone matching their descriptions. Yes, she said, five such men had spent Tuesday night with her and left very early the next morning heading up Current River. It was not good news. The train robbers were now more than twenty-four hours ahead! Tired and discouraged, the search party decided to quit the trail temporarily and go north to Licking, Missouri, for food and rest. Perhaps things would look better in the morning, they thought.

But things didn't. It was reported that during the night while the posse slept, the outlaw gang had been spotted riding west near Roubidoux about eleven miles beyond the Big Piney.[8] The train robbers were continuing to gain distance, and the posse knew that catching them was now highly unlikely. After breakfast Friday morning, the pursuers took a long hard look at their situation. Four of them decided it was time to turn back—and did.[9] The remaining seven were somehow determined to go on, for awhile at least. Having finished their business in Licking, the seven set out once again, probably taking the county road southwest toward Good Hope. However, they too soon gave up the chase and headed home.

Meanwhile, Jesse James and his gang, still occasionally stopping at farmhouses to eat, sleep, or steal fresh horses, continued their homeward journey. If they were indeed still being followed, it was now by irate farmers hunting horse thieves, not by the Gads Hill vigilance committee.

Eventually, the outlaws passed across upper Wright County and, on the morning of February 12, were seen crossing the Atlantic and Pacific railroad tracks at Brush Creek in Laclede County. They were then about three miles northeast of Phillipsburg and moving in the direction of the Bolivar road.[10]

By that time their pace had slowed dramatically. The posse was no longer trailing them and they knew it. Instead of advancing at the rate of twenty or more miles per day, as earlier in their retreat, they were now averaging only about six or seven. Perhaps they had finally reached the edge of what Frank James called the "good country" and were holing up for extended periods at the homes of old war comrades. Whatever the case, reported sightings became less frequent—then stopped. Six days passed. Nothing. Then, at shortly past midnight Wednesday morning, February 18, the train robbers were observed traveling through Bolivar in Polk County. A citizen reported that he and his wife "were awakened by the sound of horses' feet, and saw them as they filed along the middle of the street." They were then traveling in a westerly direction, he said.

The Bolivar newspaper believed that the outlaws were bound for St. Clair County. It was a reasonable assumption, because although the Younger brothers were reared in Cass and Jackson counties, they had many close friends in St. Clair and spent much time there, particularly in the vicinity of Monegaw Springs, Roscoe, and Osceola. Among those friends was Owen Snuffer, who had been a wartime associate of Cole Younger. Another was Owen's father, Theodrick. The senior Snuffer had known the boys' grandfather, Charles Lee Younger. Others who would take the brothers in included John and Hannah McFerrin, a black couple who lived in a two-story log house in the McFerrin Negro Settlement, a small community located less than three miles north of Roscoe. "Aunt Hannah," as she was called, knew the boys through her sister, who had once worked as a maid for the Younger family in Jackson County.[11]

Period maps show a crossroad about eight miles west of Bolivar and fourteen miles below the St. Clair county line. Logically, the five men would have turned at that intersection and proceeded north toward Osceola. The fact that no more sightings were reported from that point suggests they may have parted company in St. Clair County—the two Youngers stopping at the home of a friend; the James brothers and the fifth man riding on.

In upper St. Clair County the Ozark foothills give way to rolling prairie land, which continues into the counties of Henry,

Cass, Jackson, and Clay. Now traveling by road, the remaining three likely took this general course home. The long horseback ride from Gads Hill required several weeks, and it was early March before the hats of Frank and Jesse James were again hanging in their mama's parlor outside Kearney, Missouri.

PART IV

The Pursuit

Jesse James astride his horse "Stonewall." This photograph is believed to have been taken in the spring of 1874 while Jesse and his bride, Zee, were honeymooning in Sherman, Texas. At that time money from the Gads Hill train robbery was still jingling in Jesse's pockets. (Courtesy of the James Farm Museum, Kearney, Missouri)

CHAPTER 14

The Murder of Detective Whicher

The Post-office officials, the Adams Express Company, and the Iron Mountain Railroad, finally placed the matter in the hands of Allan Pinkerton, the well-known detective of this city. It was at last concluded that the five men concerned in the robbery were the famous James and Younger brothers, the former living in Clay County, and the latter in St. Clair County, in Missouri.
—*Chicago Tribune*, March 21, 1874

The long ride of the Gads Hill train robbers was at last over. Or perhaps it would be more fitting to say, they had at last reached their destination. In fact, the ride of the James and Younger brothers was never truly over. The old farm home in Clay County, which had once been a safe haven for Frank and Jesse during their boyhood years, was now only another brief stopping place in their perpetual game of hide-and-seek with the law. They were home but not "safe at home." Here, as elsewhere, it was necessary to remain ever vigilant to the encroachment of their enemies. With guns and horses close at hand, they were constantly prepared for fight or flight at a moment's notice.

Frank James described this unpleasant existence years later, just prior to his surrender. It was, he said, a "life of taut nerves, of night-riding and day-hiding, of constant listening for footfalls, crackling twigs, rustling leaves and creaking doors . . . of seeing Judas on the face of every friend."[1]

The hunt for these men, no doubt inspired by hefty reward offers, was perhaps now more intense than at any previous time in their outlaw careers. Local lawmen, detectives, and even ordinary citizens had armed themselves and taken up the chase. When the *St. Louis Dispatch* named Arthur McCoy and the James and Younger brothers as the Gads Hill bandits, it made this dire prediction: "For the first time the State has offered a reward for the bodies of the men *dead or alive*, and this may lead to renewed attempts to capture them. That they will not be taken alive if hunted down is a foregone conclusion, and that even should the attacking party succeed in bringing their dead bodies to the State Capital, it is equally certain that several vacancies will have occurred in their ranks before the desired end is accomplished."[2]

During one bloody week in March, the Dispatch's prophecy would begin to come true. Two agents of the Pinkerton National Detective Agency and a former deputy sheriff of St. Clair County would fall in quest of the outlaws—one apparently murdered by the James brothers, the other two killed in an exchange of gunfire with Jim and John Younger. In this latter scrap John Younger would lose his life as well.

The first Pinkerton employee to make the obituaries was Joseph W. Whicher, described posthumously as "one of Allan Pinkerton's best men, a cool cautious American with a great deal of experience in Western service."[3] The twenty-six-year-old detective, who had only recently married, left his bride in Iowa City and traveled to Missouri on a mission to track down the men who had robbed the train at Gads Hill. Whicher dreamed of doing what no man nor group of men had been able to do for the past eight years—capture the notorious Frank and Jesse James. Instead, the hunter himself would become the prey.

Tuesday, March 10, Whicher arrived at Liberty, the seat of Clay County. According to a *Kansas City Times* report:

> He was well dressed and made no secret of his business and his intentions. He said that he was after the Gads Hill train robbers, and that he had trailed them from Gads Hill to Clay county, and he intended to arrest the James brothers before he got through

with the job. He walked about town during the day, making close inquiries concerning whereabouts of the farm of the Widow James and the habits and customs of the James boys.[4]

Investigating authorities later insisted that the *Times* account was incorrect, that Whicher's behavior during his brief stay in Liberty was instead very secretive and professional and that he had in fact revealed himself and his mission to only two men, both prominent and trustworthy citizens.

One of these gentlemen was D. J. Adkins, president of the Commercial Savings Bank. Whicher went to the bank and introduced himself. He told Mr. Adkins he had come to the county to arrest the James boys and proceeded to detail exactly how he planned to accomplish the daring deed. He would go that very evening to their mother's farm disguised as a transient farm hand in search of work. Once employed he would await the right opportunity and, when it came, draw his pistol and nab the unsuspecting brothers on the spot.

If indeed the young Pinkerton agent had been exercising caution up to that point, it seemed certain he was now about to throw it to the wind. Adkins pleaded with him not to attempt the task alone. "They will kill you," he reportedly said. "They are dangerous people, and you want to keep away from there."[5] Whicher was undaunted by the banker's fatherly advice and pressed him for information about the men he sought. Where did they live? What did they look like? What were their habits?

Seeing that Whicher was bound and determined to go through with the risky scheme and being unable to answer adequately all his questions concerning the outlaw brothers, Adkins suggested they send for a local authority on the subject, Col. Oliver Perry Moss, former sheriff of Clay County. When Moss arrived, the three went into a back room and the discussion resumed.

Moss sided with Adkins, and he, too, made efforts to dissuade Whicher from going alone to the James farm. Even if the boys didn't kill him, he insisted, "the old woman" would. Despite the pleadings of these older and wiser heads, Whicher was still convinced he could outwit the brothers and succeed in their capture. Reluctantly, Moss answered his questions, gave descriptions of Frank and Jesse, and told him how to get to the James farm. The detective then deposited fifty dollars and his papers with the banker and gave instructions where the items were to be sent should he fail to return. He was, as the *Hamilton News* later commented, about to "[run] his head into the lion's den, fully appreciating the character of the men with whom he had to deal."[6]

It might be pointed out that it was never Allan Pinkerton's idea that Whicher should attempt a single-handed capture of the Gads Hill bandits. Nor was it likely Whicher's intention, initially. His assignment was to locate the robbers, set up a headquarters in their area where he could closely observe their comings and goings, and, when the time seemed right, get assistance and proceed with their arrest. But Whicher evidently changed his plans. The *Hamilton News* theorized: "He had been following them for several weeks with the pertinacity of a bloodhound, and perhaps the fresh trail made him too eager to close in with his game."[7]

Young Whicher, excited about the daring mission that lay before him, returned to his hotel room and waited. At 5:15 P.M., now attired in the modest garb of a farm laborer, he boarded a slow-moving freight train on the Hamilton & St. Joseph Railroad and started north for the little village of Kearney, a distance of twelve miles. The train arrived about dusk. Folks in the neighborhood later recalled seeing Whicher walking along the road in the direction of the James farm. At Kearney he was only three miles from the "lion's den."

The general public would see Whicher only once more, alive. Very early the next morning the detective, then on horseback, made an appearance at Owen's ferry landing on the Missouri River at Blue Mills. He was bound and gagged and in the company of three other men. The *Kansas City Times* gave this haunting account of what transpired at the ferry:

> One of the ferrymen was awakened at three o'clock on Wednesday morning by a party of four mounted men. One of these was a prisoner and rode a gray horse; the others rode two

bays and a sorrel horse. They commanded the ferryman to take them over the river. The man stated that it was against the rules to cross at night, and was unable to row the flatboat over the river alone. They then commenced to call across the river for the other ferryman, who was asleep in his home on the Jackson county shore.

The ferryman at first refused to go over the river, but the men notified him if he did not they would cut his boat loose and send it down the river. In reply to his question as to who they were and what they wanted, they shouted back that they were a sheriff's posse in charge of Deputy Sheriff Jim Baxter, and that they had captured a thief and were going over to Jackson county after another one. The ferryman says he knew Jim Baxter was not there, but to save his boat from going down the river he got into his skiff and rowed over to the Clay county shore. All of the horses were blanketed, the three men had their faces covered up to the eyes with woolen comforters, and their hats were drawn down as if for the purpose of concealing their identity. Only one of the men spoke, and he gave all the directions and led the bound prisoner upon the flatboat, and the party crossed over in strict silence. The prisoner did not appear to be at all restless, nor did he manifest any anxiety about his life, which was soon to be taken from him.[8]

Unhappy that he had been rousted from his warm bed under false pretenses, the ferryman, John Brickey, scolded the men for claiming to be the law. The group's spokesman pointed to their captive and replied: "You have got this d——d horse thief to thank for all this."[9]

Some details of the crossing were reported in the *Chicago Tribune*, particularly in regard to Whicher:

The [detective] was tied on his horse by a rope fastened to his legs and passing under the horse's belly, and had his arms tied behind him at the elbows; his hat was tied on with a handkerchief. One of the men dismounted and took the prisoner from his horse. Brickey says that the prisoner took things very coolly, and stamped his feet as if to warm them by restoring the circulation. Not a word was said all the way across the river. The ferryman saw that all the men except the prisoner had the lower part of their faces covered with mufflers, and their hats slouched down over their faces.

When the south side of the river was reached one of the men asked what the fare was, paid it, and the party rode off without a word. When Brickey got back to his house the clock struck 3.

As for the unfortunate detective:

On Wednesday morning, a man going to Liberty with a load of wood found Whicher's dead body lying at the meeting of the Lexington, Liberty, and Independence roads. He was shot through the temple, through the neck, and in the shoulder. A fourth shot, evidently fired by a man on horse-back, passed between his legs and was found in the ground. The pistol with which he was shot through the head was held so close as to burn the handkerchief with which his hat was tied on, while his neck was also badly burned from the close discharge of a pistol.[10]

Pinned to Whicher's breast was a note that read: "This to all detectives."[11]

Years later, Cole Younger said he was told by the men who killed Whicher that their initial intention had been to shoot him in Kansas City and leave his body on the streets. Their plans abruptly changed a few miles after crossing into Jackson County, he said, when they heard the sound of a wagon approaching on the frozen ground. It being nearly daybreak by that time, and not wishing to be seen with their captive, the men decided to finish the job then and there. Cole did not reveal who the killers were, but did imply that Jesse James was among them.[12]

Soon after Whicher's death, citizens of Jackson County claimed to have spotted his murderers. The *Kansas City Times* reported:

One of the party was seen at daylight in Independence, at the public spring. He was riding a sorrel horse, and was leading a gray answering to the description of the one ridden by the detective from Owen's ferry. The other two were seen in Kansas City on the same day.[13]

Lawmen on the case stated that before the morning was over, all three killers had returned to Clay County over the Kansas City bridge. This statement was bolstered by a report that Jesse James was seen in Kearney later in the day.

The *Hamilton News* learned the following information from Deputy Sheriff Thompson: "On the Sunday following [the murder] the deputy sheriff of Clay county went to the James farm with a posse of men and saw about the house tracks of several freshly shod horses and other indications that the gang had been at the place very recently. From the description given by the ferryman of the parties whom he took across the river, Mr. Thompson, the deputy sheriff, thinks they were Jesse James, Arthur McCoy and Jim Anderson, brother of the noted desperado, Bill Anderson."[14]

The accuracy of the ferryman's description seems questionable at best. The fact that his passengers were heavily dressed, had their faces obscured, and were viewed in the dark of night makes one wonder how he could have described them at all. Perhaps the deputy's statement was based more on a preconceived notion than on what the ferryman might have told him. In any case, the three men with Whicher that morning were undoubtedly his killers, and it is a safe bet that one, two, or all three were among the five who had robbed the train at Gads Hill.

Dick Liddil later offered another possibility as to who might have been the murderers. In a statement made to authorities after his surrender in 1882, the former gang member said:

> Regarding the killing of Detective Whicher, Jesse told me that he, Frank, Tom McDaniels, and Jim Cummins were at Mrs. Samuel's when Whicher came there. They captured him, and Jesse, McDaniels, and Frank rode off with him. Frank and McDaniels shot him.[15]

Many, however, considered Liddil's testimony unreliable.

What happened between the time Whicher left Kearney and his arrival with his captors at Owen's ferry will never be known for certain. Perhaps the James boys were forewarned of his coming and were lying in wait; some thought so. Or perhaps the detective attempted to arrest them and failed. Or it might have been simply that the outlaws saw through Whicher's thin disguise, noticing his pale cheeks and soft hands were not those of a farm laborer. Cole Younger wrote that the men frisked him and found "a pistol bearing Pinkerton's mark." Regardless of how Whicher was discovered or who killed him, the fact remains that the ambitious young detective was apparently as naive as he was courageous and, in underestimating his foes, lost his life.[16]

As the circumstances of Whicher's death became known, the identity of the killers was obvious to everyone. This excerpt from the *Chicago Tribune* says it all:

> There is no doubt in the minds of the people in Clay County that Whicher was murdered by the James boys. Between Kearney Station and the James place the settlers are all respectable. It is known that the James boys were at home on that Tuesday night, the first time they have been at home for a year, except for a day or two after the Iowa train robbery. On Thursday night, the 12th, the James boys rode into Kearney and threatened four persons, saying to them, "If you don't stop your G-d d——d talking about this murder, and connecting our names with it, we will blow your d——d head off."[17]

Clay County was apparently also buzzing about the likely connection its native sons had to the Gads Hill train robbery. The *St. Louis Globe* reported that on Friday, March 13, the brothers confronted two or three local citizens on the matter and, not in subtle terms, suggested they find safer topics of conversation.[18] The citizens no doubt complied.

In Chicago, Allan Pinkerton was notified of the tragedy and dispatched one of his men to Clay County to investigate the incident and bring back Whicher's remains. The agent's name, appropriately enough, was L. E. Angell. On the evening of March 19, the train carrying Whicher's body and its guardian, Angell, made a brief stopover in St. Louis, where it was met by a news reporter. Detective Angell gave this final tribute to his fallen colleague: "I want you to say that Whicher went down there and fell like a brave man. He leaves a young wife, and his only legacy is an honorable name . . . he died like a brave man in the discharge of his duty."[19]

Joseph Whicher's death would be just the first related to the Gads Hill train robbery.

CHAPTER 15

Pinkertons Visit St. Clair County

It is not likely that another Chicago or St. Louis detective will attempt to take the Gads Hill murderers single-handed. The fate of Mr. Whicher is an intimation they don't intend to be taken or annoyed without a determined resistance.
—*Kansas City Times,* March 14, 1874

While Detective Whicher had been pursuing Frank and Jesse James in Clay County, other agents a hundred miles to the south were hard on the trail of the Younger brothers. A St. Clair County news correspondent wrote: "Ever since the Gads Hill robbery it seems that there has been a perfect chain of detectives throughout this country tracing up the perpetrators." Among these detectives were two of Pinkerton's finest, Capt. Louis J. Lull and John H. Boyle. At some point in time the two men had formed a partnership and were now in hot pursuit of the robbery suspects.

Lull, age twenty-six, hailed originally from Vermont. In his teen years he had served as a Union soldier and more recently as a captain with the Chicago Police Department. Lull held the latter position until a recent change in administration forced his resignation. After working briefly as a hotel detective, he was approached by the Pinkertons with a more lucrative job offer.[1] Lull's partner, Boyle, was said to be a native of Maryland and had fought on the side of the Confederacy.[2] Boyle now resided in St. Louis and according to one account was once employed as a detective in that city's police force. Both men were seasoned professionals and well qualified for their present assignment.

After considerable roaming about western Missouri and searching for clues in their quest for the Gads Hill bandits, these two capable sleuths at last turned their attention to central St. Clair County, an area known to be friendly to the Youngers.

At the time of the Pinkertons' visit, Cole and Bob Younger, the oldest and youngest of the four brothers, were supposedly visiting out of state, but the other two, James, age twenty-six, and John, age twenty-three, were in St. Clair County moving about freely and mingling with the public. Although they were generally well liked in the community, these two young men did have a few enemies thereabouts; and those enemies knew not to trifle with them. Train robbery aside, during the war Jim Younger had ridden as a Confederate guerrilla with "Bloody Bill" Anderson and was thoroughly skilled in the use of firearms. Brother John also knew guns and at that particular time was wanted by authorities in the state of Texas for murdering a Dallas County sheriff. The Pinkertons were treading on dangerous ground, and they knew it.

It would later be said that on one occasion during their wanderings, the Youngers and detectives came face to face, neither party knowing the other. The men were soon to meet again. This time their meeting would not be so uneventful.

Sometime after the first week of March, the Pinkertons arrived at the county seat, Osceola. Posing as cattle buyers, they registered at the Commercial Hotel using assumed names. Boyle signed in as James Wright; Captain Lull took the alias W. J. Allen. (For purposes of this narrative, the agents will hereafter be referred to by those aliases, Wright and Allen.)

Being strangers to the area, the detectives decided to hire a guide and so added a third member to their search team, a local man named Edwin B. Daniels. This thirty-year-old native of Boston had served during the Civil War in the First Regiment of the Massachusetts Volunteer Cavalry. He now lived in Osceola, Missouri, as did his parents, who had moved there in 1866.[3] Daniels would fit nicely into their scheme, the Pinkertons thought. He was well acquainted with the county and most of its people and had frequently served as deputy sheriff. Not only would he be map and compass to the detectives but an extra gun as well.

Monday, March 16, aliases Wright and Allen and their new recruit, Daniels, rode southwest out of Osceola for Roscoe, a thriving little village on the Osage River about twelve miles distant. The three arrived in midafternoon and checked into the Roscoe House on Main Street. From this hotel headquarters they planned to set out the next day to search for the Younger brothers, who they believed had participated in the Gads Hill train robbery.

As the detectives slept soundly Monday night in their hotel room, Jim and John Younger were attending a community dance a few miles upriver at Monegaw Springs. After the dance the brothers rode down to the McFerrin Negro Settlement to spend the remaining hours of the night at the home of their black friends, John and Hannah McFerrin.

It was a typical mid-March night. The sky was star filled. The air was crisp and cool. Spring peepers were serenading in nearby woods heralding the coming new season. Somewhere in the distance a neighbor's dog barked. For a few hours the county of St. Clair rested in peaceful slumber, and all was well with the world. Then came the new day, Tuesday, March 17.

CHAPTER 16

Deadly Gunfight near Roscoe

Just then [Allen] felt the bullet in his side, and his head began to whirl. Fearing he should fall he spurred his horse into the brush, and had gone but a little way when he was knocked off the saddle by the limb of a tree.

—*St. Louis Globe,* April 3, 1874 (correspondence from the *Chicago Inter-Ocean*)

The Pinkerton men rose early Tuesday morning, St. Patrick's Day, and ate a leisurely breakfast. Later, accompanied by Daniels, they mounted their horses and struck out north from Roscoe on the road leading toward Chalk Level. They had learned through inquiry that a widow Sims had some cattle for sale, and as purchasing cattle was their pretended mission, they started in the general direction of her farm. It was not Mrs. Sims' livestock that interested these sly detectives, of course, but rather Mrs. Sims' neighbors. A number of them were known to have ridden with Cole Younger during the war, and others were long-time friends of the Younger family. The detectives concluded that some of these good folks might be well worth investigating.

Their first stop would be at the home of seventy-four-year-old Theodrick Snuffer, a gentleman who had known three generations of Youngers and whose son, Owen, had fought alongside Cole at the Battle of Lone Jack.[1] The men turned their horses east onto the road leading past Snuffer's farm, and somewhere along the way Wright separated from his two companions. The reason is unclear. One account claimed they passed the home of L. H. Brown, an acquaintance of Wright's from Maryland, and, as the detective stopped to chat, Allen and Daniels rode on.[2] Another story suggested that Wright may have served with some of these St. Clair County boys during the war and laid back for fear that someone at the Snuffer home might recognize him. Or perhaps the real reason was the one later given by Detective Allen; Wright, he said, didn't go to Snuffer's simply because he was afraid.[3] In any case, at shortly past 2:00 P.M. when Allen and Daniels approached the Snuffer farmhouse, Wright was not with them.

As the two men rode up to the front gate, they made a quick survey of the house and grounds. There was nothing to be concerned about here, they thought; but they were wrong. Unbeknownst to the detectives, two saddled horses were hidden in the barn, and Jim and John Younger were inside the house eating "dinner" less than a pistol shot away! The Snuffer home was at that moment a virtual hornet nest, and the Pinkertons were about to poke it with a stick.

When Allen and Daniels called to the house, the boys jumped to their feet nearly choking on their food. As they watched from a place of concealment, old Mr. Snuffer, faking calm, hobbled out to greet the visitors. The men were looking to buy cattle, or so they claimed, and needed directions to the Sims place. Snuffer pointed the way. After a brief conversation, they thanked the old man and left. Snuffer went back inside as the boys continued to observe the departing horsemen from a parlor window. Soon after, a third rider (Wright) passed the house and overtook the two. The Youngers, already suspicious, became even more so when the men failed to follow Snuffer's directions. Instead of continuing on to the next road and turning back east toward the Sims place, they rode a short distance and turned northwest up a logging road. There was now no longer any doubt in the minds of Jim and John Younger; these "cattle buyers" were, in truth, detectives on the prowl, and the Younger boys were their intended prey. It was quickly concluded by the brothers that they, the pursued, should now become the pursuers, and mounting their horses, they set out on the hunt.

The detectives were barely past the McFerrin Negro Settlement when Jim and John Younger suddenly came riding up from behind with guns drawn. At the time, Daniels and Allen were riding side by side, with Wright a few yards in advance. Wright was acting very nervous, Allen later told a reporter; he kept his horse "fretting" and was constantly looking over his shoulder. It was he who first saw the approaching outlaws. "Who's that coming?" he wanted to know. Daniels looked back and whispered, "By G-d, those are the Youngers!"[4] Wright didn't stop to say hello. Quick as a flash he spurred his mount and, as one newspaper put it, "ran like a quarterhorse."[5] The Youngers shouted for Wright to halt and fired, reportedly shooting off his hat, but he continued at full gallop.

Daniels and Allen stopped and faced the outlaws. Jim Younger was armed with revolvers. John carried a double-barreled shotgun, both hammers cocked, and had a dragoon revolver under his leg on the saddle. The detectives were ordered to remove their pistols and drop them on the road. Holding Daniels and Allen at bay with the shotgun, John Younger told his brother to go after Wright and bring him back. Jim refused. Instead, he dismounted and picked up the discarded weapons, one dropped by Daniels and two by Allen. After a close examination, Jim remarked that they were "damn fine pistols" and insisted their captives make presents of them. The gunfight that followed was described at the coroner's inquest by a mortally wounded Captain Lull, still using the alias W. J. Allen:

> One of them then asked me where we came from, and I said from Osceola; he then wanted to know what we were doing in this part of the country; I replied, rambling around. One of them then said, you were up here one day before; I replied that we were not; he then said we had been at the Springs; I replied, we had been at the Springs, but had not been inquiring for them, that we did not know them, and they said detectives had been up there hunting for them all the time, and they were going to stop it. Daniels then said, "I am no detective; I can show you who I am and where I belong"; and one of them said he knew him, and then turned to me and said, "What in the hell are you riding around here with

all them pistols on for?" and I said: "Good God! is not every man wearing them that is traveling and have I not as much right to wear them as any one else?" and the one that had the shot gun said, "Hold on, young man, we don't want any of that," and then lowered the gun, cocked, in a threatening manner.

Detective Allen, no doubt remembering the recent murder of his colleague, Whicher, decided to take drastic action. "I concluded that they intended to kill us," he recalled. "I reached my hand behind me and drew a No. 2 Smith & Wesson pistol and cocked it and fired at the one on horseback."

Allen's shot was on the mark. The small-caliber bullet tore through the right side of John Younger's neck, grazing the upper part of his clavicle bone and coming out the other side. John immediately answered with blasts from both barrels of his shotgun, shattering Allen's left arm and causing him to drop the reins. During the confusion brother Jim instinctively opened fire on Daniels, who fell wounded from his horse and died almost instantly.

Allen's horse, frightened by the gunfire, bolted with its rider and fled down the road. Although himself mortally wounded,

The road near Roscoe, Missouri, where Pinkerton detectives were confronted by Jim and John Younger in 1874. The McFerrin cabin stood about a hundred feet off the road to the left.

This stone marker, erected in 1934, stands near the site of the gun battle.

John Younger drew a pistol and gave chase. Moments later he overtook the horse and rider and fired on Allen at close range—one shot missing, the other piercing the detective's left side. Allen testified:

> I lost all control of my horse, and he turned into the brush and a small tree struck me and knocked me out of the saddle. I then got up and staggered across the road and lay down until I was found. No one else was present.[6]

This part of the gunfight was witnessed by John McFerrin and one of his sons. The McFerrin cabin, where Jim and John Younger had spent the night, stood a short distance east of where the shooting commenced. McFerrin heard the shots, he said, and soon after saw two riders racing down the road, one in pursuit of the other. As they rode past his house he recognized the pursuer as John Younger. McFerrin testified, "I think they were both shooting at one another; I am certain that John Younger was shooting at the other man; he continued to run down the road east of here; I think John Younger passed the man on the gray horse; about the time John Younger passed him I saw him [Allen] sink on his horse, as if going to fall; don't know what become of him afterwards; then Younger turned to come west and began to sink, and then fell off his horse."[7]

As John Younger fell, he went over a low fence and landed face down in a hog pen, his life's blood rapidly ebbing away. Jim hurried down the road on foot and knelt beside his dying brother. The *Bolivar Free Press* reported, "A farmer who lived near the scene of the conflict, and witnessed it in part, testified that when the shooting was over, and John Younger had fallen from his horse, James Younger came up to him, raised him up and asked, 'Can you see me?' John made no reply and died in a minute after."[8]

Another witness to the running fight was George W. ("Speed") McDonald, a son-in-law of the McFerrins. He stated that he also had seen the two men riding down the road "shooting at each other." According to his statement, "John Younger fell from his horse; James Younger came running up to where John had fallen and called me to him; he then turned him (John Younger) over and took some revolvers off of him, and a watch and something else out of his pockets; I don't know what else . . . ; I think James Younger took four revolvers off of John Younger, his brother; he threw one over the fence and told me to keep it; he then told me to catch a horse and go down and tell Snuffer's folks."[9]

Before taking to the brush, Jim, stunned and grief stricken, decided to break the bad news to the Snuffer family himself. According to the *Free Press,* he "mounted a horse and rode to Snuffer's where the two had eaten dinner, gave some directions about the funeral, and disappeared, stating that he was going to leave St. Clair county forever."[10]

The coroner's jury reached a verdict. John Younger, it was concluded, "came to his death by a pistol shot, supposed to have been in the hands of W. J. Allen." And Edwin Daniels "came to his death by a pistol shot, supposed to have been fired by the hand of James Younger."[11]

CHAPTER 17

Aftermath of the Battle

There was much excitement throughout St. Clair county, last week, over the tragedy, and some talk was expressed in the vicinity of the conflict that the end was not yet.

—*Bolivar Free Press,* March 26, 1874

After the shooting, local farmfolk continued to gather. Ed Daniels was dead in the road, and John Younger, also dead, lay in the hog pen across the road from McFerrin's cabin. Both had died of neck wounds.

Detective Allen was still conscious, although he was bleeding and in great pain. His left arm and wrist had been peppered with close-range buckshot, and a bullet had passed through the lower part of his left lung.[1] When the farmers approached, he was uncertain of their motives and feigned death. His act was not convincing. One of the crowd, obviously a friend of the Youngers, suggested they finish him off, but the others disagreed.[2] A white farmer, John Davis, whose son had witnessed part of the shooting, assured Allen that he had fallen into good hands and would not be harmed.[3] The wounded detective was then gently carried to the front porch of McFerrin's cabin, where he was tended until a wagon could be prepared to transport him back to Roscoe. That evening he was taken to the Roscoe House and placed under the immediate care of the town doctor, forty-one-year-old A. C. Marquis. For the next several

John and Hannah McFerrin in front of the cabin where Jim and John Younger slept the night prior to their gunfight with the Pinkertons. It was onto this front porch that mortally wounded Capt. Louis Lull (alias W. J. Allen) and the body of Edwin Daniels were carried after the fight. John Younger's body was later taken inside the house and guarded overnight. (Courtesy of the State Historical Society of Missouri, Columbia)

weeks, the little hotel room would be a virtual hospital room as doctors worked to save Allen's life.

When word of the gunfight reached Osceola, via Detective Wright, friends of Ed Daniels mounted at once and rode out to learn his fate. They soon returned with the sad news that both Daniels and John Younger were dead.

As details of the tragedy unfolded and it was learned that Allen had pulled a hidden pistol and initiated the shooting, Daniels' friends were outraged. The Youngers had not intended to harm the detectives, they insisted; the boys only wanted to talk. Ed was murdered, his friends said, because a "d——d fool Chicago blow-hard did not know what danger he was in." The journalist reporting the story agreed. "Not a man would have been harmed," he wrote, "but for the stupidity or nervousness of Allen, the Chicago detective." The general contention was that if Allen had meant to fight, he should have done so at the outset, not after he and Daniels had been disarmed.[4]

In a short while the crowd at the McFerrin Negro Settlement grew even larger. Tension was mounting, and Sheriff James R. Johnson ordered his deputy, Simpson Beckley, and a posse of armed volunteers to ride out and calm things down. But when word came that the wounded detective had been taken to Roscoe and all other parties involved were either dead or had fled the scene, Beckley and his men rode instead to the Roscoe House. Fearing potential retaliation against Allen from the Younger brothers or their friends, the deputy and his volunteers were placed on guard overnight around the hotel.

That same evening a hack was sent to transport Daniels' body home to his grieving parents in Osceola. Three days later the popular ex-deputy would be given a hometown funeral and be buried in the Osceola Cemetery.

The body of John Younger was placed inside McFerrin's cabin and guarded overnight by a seventeen-year-old farm youth named David Crowder.[5] There was apparently some fear that

The old McFerrin cabin as it appeared in later years. (Illustration by author from a photograph courtesy of Wilbur A. Zink)

John Younger, killed March 17, 1874, during the gunfight with Pinkerton detectives. (Courtesy of the State Historical Society of Missouri, Columbia)

The grave of John Younger stands out from all the others in Yeater Cemetery because of its unusual angle. John was buried with his head to the northwest and his feet to the southeast.

enemies of the Youngers might make an attempt to mutilate the corpse or cart it off. Early Thursday morning it was buried in a shallow grave near the Snuffer farmhouse and that night secretly dug up by Mr. Snuffer and George McDonald and given a permanent burial a few miles away in Yeater Cemetery. Still fearing body snatchers, they left the grave unmarked but deliberately dug at an angle, northwest to southeast, so that family and friends would be able to identify it. The grave was never molested. It is today marked by a gray, granite tombstone that can be readily identified because of its conspicuous angle.

Back in Roscoe the wounded Detective Allen remained under strict medical care. His wife and mother had traveled down from Chicago to help care for him, and one of their first acts was to replace Dr. Marquis with a more experienced physician, Dr. D. C. McNeill. Also there from Chicago was Detective R. J. Linden, assigned by the Pinkerton Agency to serve as nurse and guard to the fallen agent.

A rumor soon circulated in the community that Cole Younger was swearing vengeance against his brother's slayer; Allen would never get out of the county alive, he promised. Whether this was true or not, the possibility existed, and the detective was guarded around the clock. According to the *Chicago Times,* even Allen's wife armed herself with a revolver.[6]

The Pinkertons now no longer found it necessary to conceal the injured man's identity. "Allen" had been using an alias, they finally admitted; his real name was in fact Louis J. Lull, and he was a former captain with the Chicago police. As to his medical condition, they remained tight-lipped.

On March 22 the *Chicago Tribune* erroneously reported that Lull had died. Several other newspapers printed the story as well but later had to retract. The sturdy captain continued to cling to life, and for a time it seemed as though he might recover. Toward the end of April, Mrs. Lull mailed a letter to her brother in Chicago stating that her husband would soon be well enough to come home, maybe even in time to celebrate his twenty-seventh birthday, May 16. But, sadly, it was not to be. Just a week after the letter was received, Captain Lull took a turn for the worse. At 7:45 on the evening of May 6, with his wife of nine months, his mother, brother, and Detective Linden at his bedside, he slipped quietly away. A telegram sent to his mother-in-law read:

> Roscoe, Mo., May 6.—To Mrs. CATHARINE POWER, 143 N. Ada street: Louis is dead. Will bury in Chicago.
>
> R. J. LINDEN[7]

Louis J. Lull (alias W. J. Allen) was laid to rest in Chicago's Rose Hill Cemetery with Masonic honors. Pinkerton agents attended his funeral, and a large number of Chicago police officers were on hand to pay final respects.

And what became of Mr. Wright, the agent who turned white feather and left his companions to fend for themselves? The frightened detective, no doubt inspired by the bullet that knocked off his hat, had continued spurring his horse at full gallop. He did not care where he was going as long as it was away from the Youngers. As more gunfire popped behind him, Wright felt certain that Allen and Daniels were being slaughtered and that the outlaws would be coming after him next. He turned right onto the Chalk Road and proceeded at top speed until he came to a farmer and son who were cutting wood near the road. Reining to a stop, he pulled a greenback from his pocket and offered to buy the older man's hat. The deal was quickly made. It was a farmer's work hat, but style was not important to Wright at the moment. He knew that the Youngers, if they came, would be looking for a bareheaded rider. Now hatted once again and feeling less conspicuous, the detective changed course and eventually made his way safely back to Osceola, where he reported the shooting to Sheriff Johnson.[8]

Most people perceived Wright's fleeing the scene as an act of cowardice, but he had an explanation. The three of them had agreed at the outset, he said, that in the event of an attack they were to be "on the fly" and it would be every man for himself.[9] Whether or not this was truly the agreed plan, it was Wright's plan, and the moment the Youngers hollered "halt" he executed it perfectly.

Wright supposedly told a different story to the *Chicago Inter-Ocean*. In that version he didn't flee until the shooting started—and even then it was his horse's idea, not his. The horse, frightened by the gunfire, bolted and started running down the road with Wright having no choice but to go along for the ride. According to Wright, Jim Younger mounted and gave chase. The newspaper reported, "When [Wright] found Jim pursuing him he turned his horse into the thicket, lost his hat, which, he says, was shot from his head (but it has no bullet marks), and never halted till he reached Osceola, seven miles away."[10]

There was really very little Wright could say or do to change the public's negative opinion of him. He had deserted his friends when they needed him most—and they had been gunned down while he escaped unscathed.

Sometime after reporting the shooting, Wright quietly slipped out of Osceola and made his way twenty-some miles northwest to

Appleton City, where he laid low until the Pinkerton superintendent in St. Louis telegraphed him to come home.

On the morning of March 23, Wright boarded the eastbound train for St. Louis. His journey home was not a pleasant one. Not only was he racked with guilt for having deserted his comrades, but the paranoid detective felt certain that one of the outlaw gang was on the train following him.

That evening a lone *St. Louis Dispatch* reporter stood on the platform at the Seventh Street depot in St. Louis awaiting arrival of the 6:40 train. He had learned that the Pinkerton man who had recently escaped the wrath of the Younger brothers was to be on board and was eager to get an interview. On the platform with him was Tommy Smith, a security policeman. As the two conversed, the train came rolling in.

The reporter had no idea what Wright looked like and was concerned about how he might pick him out of the crowd of debarking passengers. As it turned out, the detective revealed himself immediately. Here, through the eyes of the news reporter, we get a close-up look at the nervous little man who called himself James Wright:

> The train was on time, and Tommy Smith, as well as the reporter who stood guard at the outlet from the platform, "piped off" the passengers. Before the train came to a stop a small man jumped off, and running up to the officer whispered something in his ear, but Smith did not have time to attend to him. He appeared to be very excited. Conductor Baker came next, and the reporter introduced himself, at the same time stating his mission.
>
> "Here's a gentleman wants to see you," said the gentlemanly conductor to the excited individual, who approached warily.
>
> "Being a reporter, I should like very much to get a correct version of the chase of the Youngers from you," mildly suggested the newspaper man at the same time closely scrutinizing the man who ran.
>
> He bore a striking resemblance to Canada Bill, king of the monte men, only a couple of sizes smaller and more youthful in appearance. His features are very sharp and his eyes very bright and penetrating. He is low of stature and stoops considerably. Attired in top boots, light coat, minus a shirt collar and with a black hat slouched over his eyes the detective looked not unlike a farmer just returned from a hunt after his cattle.

His reply to the query propounded by the *DISPATCH* man was, "I can't be bothered with reporters."

He then button-holed Officer Smith again and informed him that, in his opinion, one of the robbers was on the train.

"Do you want him arrested?" asked Tommy.

A negative answer was returned and the officer suggested that he had better watch the omnibuses for the suspected party.

"You were mighty lucky to get away from them fellers," remarked the star [Smith].

"I don't want to talk about it, I don't want to talk about it," said the valiant cop, throwing up both hands. "They shoot both ways at once," throwing out his right and left dukes simultaneously, "and drop their man at a hundred yards." and the detective looking as if he saw, in his mind's eye, those terrible Youngers bearing down on the trio who went out to capture them.

Having delivered himself of this speech in a nervous manner the detective ran to the eastern end of the depot and disappeared, evidently fearing that the heroes of Gads Hill were still on his track.[11]

Wright may have been able to run from news reporters, but he couldn't hide. He continued to be plagued by unwanted publicity. Almost immediately there was controversy as to his real name. Some newspapers insisted it was "Duckworth," but the claim was flatly denied by the Pinkerton Agency. William Pinkerton (son of Allan) declared that the real Detective Duckworth "is in no way connected with our force, nor has he been . . . and, so far as I know, has not been interested in the Gads Hill case."[12]

Another who knew that Wright was not Duckworth—and he was even more certain—was Duckworth himself. In an April 6 interview at the Southern Hotel in St. Louis, Detective James Duckworth lamented to a reporter that the "mix-up" had caused him a great deal of harm.[13]

Eventually, it became known to one and all that the true name of the agent who fled was neither Wright nor Duckworth, but John H. Boyle.

The St. Louis Pinkerton office apparently decided to give Boyle a second chance and sent him back—this time to Clay County—to resume his search for the Gads Hill robbers. On May 12, Allan Pinkerton, still angry over Boyle's actions at

Roscoe and seeming to mistrust him for other reasons (unspecified), wrote a letter expressing those sentiments to George H. Bangs of the New York office.[14] A short time later, Detective Boyle was called back to St. Louis and fired.

Now in need of a job, the unemployed detective applied for a position with the local police department, but he made the unwise decision of giving the Pinkerton Agency as a reference. In a letter sent July 2 to Dan O'Conner, chief detective of the St. Louis police, William Pinkerton wrote that Boyle had once been an agent with his force but was discharged because of cowardice and unreliability. He blamed Boyle for Captain Lull's death, called him a "dirty dog," and advised the St. Louis Police Department to have nothing to do with him.[15] And thus, perhaps, ended the detective career of John H. Boyle (alias James Wright).

With the passing of Captain Lull, the Pinkerton-Younger gun battle became history. All that remained were grief and bitterness, emotions felt strongly by both sides. And there was the lingering question: Who was responsible for the deaths of the three men? The subject would be a major topic of conversation in the county for years to come. Some blamed Lull for pulling the hidden pistol; had he not fired the first shot, they claimed, the Youngers would have merely given the detectives a lecture and sent them on their way. Others were critical of the local man, Daniels, saying he should never have been riding with the Pinkertons in the first place. And many, of course, had unkind words to say about the agent who fled.

The outspoken widow, who for weeks had nursed and guarded Lull so diligently, blamed not only "the coward Wright" for her husband's demise but pointed an accusing finger at Dr. Marquis as well. The doctor's "ignorance and blundering" in the initial treatment of his wounds, she bluntly proclaimed, was why Captain Lull failed to survive.

In the heat of emotion many hasty opinions were formed, but, when things grew calmer, more rational minds remembered what the law never forgot: The real culprits responsible for the St. Clair County tragedy were the James-Younger outlaw gang, the robbers of the train at Gads Hill.

CHAPTER 18

Revenge

Revenge at first thought sweet,
Bitter ere long back on itself recoils.
—John Milton, *Paradise Lost*, Book VIII (1667)

The tragic chain of events spawned by the Gads Hill train robbery did not end with the shooting deaths in St. Clair County. An irate Allan Pinkerton, seething over the murders of his agents and bent on retaliation, wrote to George Bangs: "I know that the James and the Youngers are desperate men, and that when we meet it must be the death of one or both of us . . . my blood was spilt, and they must repay, there is no use talking, they must die."[1]

Frank and Jesse did repay. Nine months later, January 26, 1875, a group of Pinkerton agents came to Clay County by special train. Having been informed that the brothers were visiting their mother and stepfather at the old James homestead, the detectives crept up quietly in the night and hurled an explosive device through the kitchen window. Eight-year-old Archie Peyton Samuel, the James boys' half-brother, was killed in the blast and their mother suffered a mangled right forearm, which had to be amputated. Her wayward sons, if they were home, were not apprehended.

Immediately following the fatal assault, a hired hand named Jack Ladd, who had for several months been working on the

155

adjoining farm of Daniel Askew, disappeared from the community. It was widely believed that Ladd was a planted Pinkerton spy and that he and Askew had aided the Pinkertons in the bombing raid. On the night of April 12, Dan Askew was shot to death in the backyard of his home. Frank and Jesse James were suspected of the murder.

Six years passed and on the warm summer evening of July 15, 1881, a band of robbers, thought to have been led by the James brothers, held up a Chicago, Rock Island and Pacific express train near Winston, Missouri. Just prior to the robbery, conductor William H. Westfall was innocently collecting tickets in the smoking car. As he proceeded down the aisle, a bearded man wearing a white linen duster suddenly stood up behind him and ordered him to throw up his hands. Before the startled conductor could comply, he was shot twice in the back. Wounded and bleeding, Westfall staggered out onto the rear platform of the car and fell from the moving train, dead. To keep up the scare, two other outlaws in the car quickly rose from their seats and began randomly firing their pistols. In the fusillade a passenger, Frank McMillan, was killed by a stray bullet.

It was never determined whose shot killed McMillan, but the murder of Westfall was laid to Jesse James. Again, some said, the motive was revenge. True or not, rumors circulated that Westfall had been in charge of the special train that brought the Pinkerton men to Clay County the night of the fatal bombing.[2]

Joseph Whicher, Ed Daniels, Louis Lull, John Younger, little Archie Samuel, Daniel Askew, William Westfall, and Frank McMillan were all dead, and Mrs. Samuel had lost an arm. The Gads Hill train robbery, which some news reporters had viewed at the time as a romantic and heroic deed performed by "robber-knights," had left behind a long, not-so-romantic trail of blood and tears.

PART V

Reflections

Jesse James. Some historians say this photograph of Jesse was probably taken at Nebraska City in 1875; others believe it was made in the spring of 1874, around the time of his wedding to Zerelda (Zee) Mimms. (Courtesy of Phillip W. Steele)

Frank James at age fifty-five, about sixteen years after his surrender. (Author's collection)

Cole Younger, as he appeared during his incarceration at the Minnesota State Penitentiary, Stillwater. (Author's collection)

Jim Younger at the Minnesota State Penitentiary, Stillwater. Fifteen months after being released from prison, Jim committed suicide. (Author's collection)

Bob Younger at the Minnesota State Penitentiary, Stillwater. Ill with consumption (tuberculosis), and his appeals for release denied, Bob died in prison September 16, 1889. (Author's collection)

CHAPTER 19

Who Robbed the Gads Hill Train?

I think they are a regular set of robbers, and am positive they
are the same gang who robbed the coach at Hot Springs, and
probably were among the Iowa mail-train robbers.
—Conductor Chauncey Alford, *St. Louis Republican*,
February 2, 1874

During the days immediately following the train robbery at Gads
Hill, there were varying opinions as to who might have been the
bandits. At first, suspicions focused mostly on local riff-raff,[1] but
as the outlaw trail continued westward, suspicions shifted westward as well—all the way to the Missouri counties of Clay and St.
Clair, respective headquarters of the James and Younger brothers. By February 10 the *St. Louis Dispatch* was expressing "very little doubt . . . as to the identity of the band." Naming Arthur
McCoy, Frank and Jesse James, and the Younger brothers as the
train bandits, the newspaper went on to list several of their former associates and a number of robberies that had been attributed to them over the past eight years.[2]

The *Dispatch* claimed that McCoy was the leader at Gads
Hill. Several other newspapers reported that it was former
Quantrill lieutenant William Greenwood. Local opinion
favored Sam Hildebrand. And in faraway Chicago, the
Pinkertons maintained that Frank and Jesse James had been in

charge and that they and the Youngers were accompanied by Clell Miller and Jim Cummins.[3]

A few months later, after much of the initial excitement had died down, yet another suspect emerged—former Quantrill man James Reed. Although there was not a shred of evidence connecting him to the robbery, newspapers printed the tale, and Reed received a brief period of posthumous infamy.

When all was said and done, the suspects of Gads Hill numbered about a dozen men: Frank and Jesse James, the four Younger brothers, Jim Reed, Arthur McCoy, Clell Miller, Bill Greenwood, Jim Cummins, and Sam Hildebrand. No one was ever captured for the crime; no one ever surrendered, confessed, or stood trial. The absence of a confessor left a question that has never been fully resolved. Who were the train robbers? Let's take a brief look at each of our suspects and see what conclusions might be drawn.

Samuel S. Hildebrand

A native of St. Francois County, Missouri, Sam Hildebrand first gained notoriety during the Civil War as an irregular Confederate guerrilla leader conducting forays against Federal troops in southeastern Missouri and northeastern Arkansas. After the war he remained on the wrong side of the law and by the early 1870s was wanted for numerous murders. Among local badmen he seemed the most likely suspect.

Sam, however, had been unable to attend the Gads Hill train robbery due to a death in the family—his own. His accusers would later learn that back on March 21, 1872, Sam had been gunned down by a law officer in Pinckneyville, Illinois.[4] At the time of the train robbery the ex-bushwhacker had been moldering in his grave for nearly two years. He lies there still, in the old Hampton Cemetery in what is today Park Hills, Missouri.[5]

James Robert Cummins

Like so many boys in Clay and neighboring western Missouri counties during the Civil War, Jim Cummins (sometimes spelled Cummings) joined Quantrill's band. Because of his association with Frank and Jesse James, the Pinkertons suspected him of being at Gads Hill. That suspicion now seems to have been groundless. Although never considered particularly talented as an outlaw, Jim was greatly respected for his superb horsemanship. In interviews, his old war comrades always remembered him as "the best rider in the troop."[6]

Jim was wanted in connection with other robberies as well, but by 1898 all charges against him had been dropped, and at age fifty he became a free man. The ex-outlaw lived thirty-one more years, dying in 1929 at the Confederate Nursing Home in Higginsville, Missouri.

William Greenwood

Soon after passengers of the plundered train were interviewed in Little Rock, several newspapers across America declared that the leader of the robbers was named Greenwood. No source was given for the accusation.

The name Greenwood came up again in March 1882, when short-time gang member Dick Liddil voluntarily surrendered to authorities. Being promised a full pardon, Liddil made a lengthy confession statement telling everything he knew about the James brothers and their crimes—plus probably a few things he didn't know. One of his unconfirmed claims was that Jesse James once told him that he (Jesse), brother Frank, and William Greenwood were among the robbers at Gads Hill.[7]

During the war Greenwood served as a lieutenant with Quantrill. Besides being a natural leader, he was said to be one of the best and quickest pistol shots in the company.[8] The Jameses and Youngers no doubt knew him well and admired his talents, but their association with him after the war is questionable.

Bill Greenwood married Mary Beverly of Howard County, Missouri, sometime after 1872. In his book *Noted Guerrillas,* published in 1877, John Newman Edwards wrote that Greenwood was then a prosperous farmer living in northwestern Missouri.[9] Could it be that the downpayment on Greenwood's farm came from the Hot Springs-Gads Hill robberies?

Clelland D. Miller

According to tradition, Clell Miller was the robber who laid his overcoat on the tracks at Gads Hill prior to the train's arrival. Although there is no evidence that Clell did in fact participate in that raid, there is certainly a possibility. This former Confederate guerrilla grew up in Clay County, Missouri, as did the James boys, rode with Jesse in "Bloody Bill" Anderson's outfit, and later joined the brothers in several of their postwar exploits. During the mid-1870s he was considered one of the gang's most capable and trusted members.

Capable though he might have been, twenty-six-year-old Clell Miller was shot dead on the street, September 7, 1876, as the James-Younger gang made its infamous bank robbery attempt at Northfield, Minnesota. Instead of being buried, the body was preserved in a barrel of alcohol and shipped to a University of Michigan medical school laboratory for study. Miller's remains were eventually returned to Missouri, and the outlaw was laid to rest in Muddy Fork Cemetery in Clay County, not far from his boyhood home.[10]

Arthur C. McCoy

In the early 1870s Arthur McCoy was a well-known member of the James-Younger band and therefore suspected by many of the robbery at Gads Hill. Some contemporary newspapers even considered him the leader and dubbed these outlaws the "Arthur McCoy Gang."

McCoy did not fit the standard profile of a border outlaw. Nearly all of the boys in this group had grown up on farms in western Missouri and during the Civil War had fought as rebel guerrillas under Quantrill, Anderson, or Todd. McCoy was several years older than the other gang members, and his background was quite different, as he was neither farm boy, ex-guerrilla, nor native of western Missouri. He instead hailed from the opposite side of the state, St. Louis, and prior to the war had worked as a tinner. Joining the First Missouri Confederate Infantry, McCoy fought valiantly at the Battle of Shiloh, where his unit was nearly wiped out. He later returned to Missouri and served the remainder of the war in the cavalry unit of Gen. Joseph Shelby. His comrades there nicknamed him the "Wild Irishman" for his pluck and daring, the same qualities that eventually earned him a captain's commission.[11]

John Newman Edwards, who had served as adjutant to Shelby, remembered McCoy as being thin, more than six feet tall, with slightly stooped shoulders and long arms. His eyes were a penetrating blue, Edwards wrote, and his jaw massive and square cut. He also noted that McCoy had a dry, raspy cough and was probably consumptive.[12] Was Edwards perhaps describing the "huge six-footer" with the hoarse voice who collared conductor Alford as he stepped off the train at Gads Hill?

When, where, or how Arthur McCoy died was never officially confirmed. One news account told that he was killed in a shootout with pursuers in northern Arkansas sometime around March 1, 1874.[13] Another claim came in an anonymous letter obtained by the *St. Louis Dispatch* stating that McCoy had died of consumption in Texas, January 11, 1874, and was buried along the San Marcos River.[14] If the latter story is true, Arthur McCoy was of course not party to the Hot Springs and Gads Hill robberies as many believed.

All that is known for certain is that Arthur's name was not listed with the rest of the family in a special 1876 census of Montgomery County, Missouri, where the McCoys then owned a small farm. Later, in the 1880 census, his wife, Louisa, was listed as family head and widowed.[15]

James C. Reed

Former Missourian and Quantrill guerrilla James Reed was shot and killed August 6, 1874, by special deputy John T. Morris during an arrest attempt in northeastern Texas. As Reed lay dying, Morris later claimed, the outlaw confessed that he and his gang, not Jesse James, were the true robbers of Gads Hill. Those who believed the confession tale were probably not aware that Mr. Morris had a strong tendency to distort the truth, especially when it benefited his own public image.

On April 7 of that year, a stagecoach was held up near San Antonio, Texas, and John Morris was given special authority to go after Reed, the main suspect. Morris would later offer two different accounts of his relationship with Reed and how he did him in.

Version one, and probably the correct one, was in a sworn statement at the coroner's inquest held the day of the killing. Morris said he had been "well acquainted" with Reed and, after gaining his trust, pretended to join him in a scheme to rob an old man in Arkansas. The two were traveling horseback to that destination, he said, when they decided to stop for dinner at the home of an S. M. Harvey near Paris, Texas. Morris suggested they leave their firearms with the horses, and Reed agreed, not knowing that his friend planned to betray him. "I got done eating before Reed," Morris told the coroner, "and went back into the main room and explained to Harvey Reed's character and asked him to assist in his arrest." Harvey agreed to help, and the two secretly went out to the horses and retrieved the pistols. Morris continued:

> We went to the dining room, where Reed was still eating. I said to Reed, "Jim, throw up your hands"; he said he would do so but ran under the table and raised up with the table and ran towards the door with the table in advance. I shot two holes through the table. After he dropped the table I shot him in the right side."[16]

According to news reports, Reed was hit twice and died almost instantly. At no time during his testimony did Morris mention a deathbed statement.

Ten days later, however, perhaps to make himself appear braver and Reed more villainous, Morris wrote to newspapers telling quite a different story. In his new, improved version, Morris was not traveling with Reed at all but instead tracked the outlaw for three weeks and "came upon" him "where he had stopped for dinner." And Morris did not shoot a fleeing unarmed man, he now claimed, but had instead bravely bested him in a one-on-one gunfight. Morris wrote:

> I called upon [Reed] to surrender, and he refused, making fight and firing upon me. In that combat I wounded him mortally. He lived two hours after he was shot, making, before he died, a full confession.[17]

In this now remembered "confession," Morris claimed that with his dying breath Reed admitted not only to the San Antonio stage robbery but to a number of other well-publicized heists as well. The latter included the robberies at Gads Hill and Hot Springs; the train raid near Adair, Iowa; and the bank holdup at Ste. Genevieve, Missouri—all misdeeds usually attributed to Jesse James and his band. Except for perhaps the San Antonio stage robbery, there has never been reason to believe that Reed was guilty of any of the above crimes or, for that matter, that any such confession even took place. It appears in fact that this particular badman, even in his best years, was little more than a small-time house robber, cattle rustler, and horse thief.

(While Jim Reed never gained legendary fame as an outlaw, his widow, Myra Maebelle, did. After a brief marriage to Bruce Younger, Cole Younger's uncle, the gun-toting Myra married a Cherokee desperado named Sam Starr and became celebrated in dime novels as Belle Starr, the Bandit Queen. In 1889 Belle was shot and killed by an unknown assailant while riding her horse near her home in the Indian Territory.)

The Younger Brothers

As previously stated, the outlaw Youngers numbered four.

Thomas Coleman Younger (Cole), the oldest and largest of the brothers, was born in Jackson County, Missouri, January 15, 1844. At maturity he stood nearly six feet tall and weighed in excess of two hundred pounds.[18] During the war he held a captain's rank in Quantrill's band and later rode as an outlaw with Jesse James. According to some imaginative writers, it was Cole who returned the money to G. R. Crump during the Hot Springs stage robbery and one of the two gunmen who forced the engineer and fireman off the train at Gads Hill.

James Hardin Younger, who first saw the light of day January 15, 1848, exactly four years after Cole, was a former guerrilla as well. This somewhat quiet and moody brother rode with "Bloody Bill" Anderson. On the day the Hot Springs stage was robbed, Jim Younger was celebrating his twenty-sixth birthday; Cole, his thirtieth.

John Harrison Younger and Robert Ewing Younger, born 1851 and 1853 respectively, had been too young to serve in the war. Although lacking the horse and revolver experience of their older brothers, John and Bob may have been riding with the gang to some extent by the early 1870s.

Authorities suspected that at least two of the Youngers had been among the Gads Hill train robbers, and, when the trail eventually led pursuers to their hangout in St. Clair County, those suspicions were strongly reinforced. Cole denied any involvement in the raid and published cards stating that he and Bob had been visiting a friend in Louisiana during the time in question. A few months later, continuing to plead his case, he wrote to a brother-in-law, Lycurgus Jones, editor of the *Pleasant Hill Review*. The letter, dated November 15, 1874, offered alibis for several recent crimes, including the Hot Springs and Gads Hill robberies. Of those he wrote:

> About the 1st of December, 1873, I arrived in Carroll parish, Louisiana. I staid there until the 8th of February, 1874. I and

brother staid at Wm. Dickerson's, near Floyd. Dickerson was master of a Masonic lodge, and during the time the Shreveport stage and the Hot Springs stage were robbed; also the Gads Hill robbery. Now, if the governor or any one else wants to satisfy himself in regard to the above he can write to the Masonic fraternity, Floyd, Carroll Parish, Louisiana. I hope the leading journals will investigate the matter, and then, if they find I have misrepresented anything they can show me up to the world as being guilty, but if they find it as I have stated they surely would have no objections to state the facts as they are.[19]

William Dickerson later substantiated Cole's alibi in a letter to Augustus C. Appler, editor of the *Osceola Democrat*. Dickerson wrote that the two Younger brothers had stayed at his home from December 5, 1873, until February 8, 1874. The letter was cosigned by ten upstanding citizens of Carroll Parish, all vouching that the statements of their neighbor, Dickerson, were "true and correct."[20]

There is another reason for believing that Cole may have been telling the truth. On January 30, one day prior to the Gads Hill robbery, a merchant trade boat moored at Port Jefferson on the Boeuf River in northern Louisiana was robbed at gunpoint by five "handsomely dressed, good-looking men." They reportedly made off with about one thousand dollars in cash and goods amounting to at least five hundred dollars. The *New York Times* stated, "The robbers were strangers in that section, and are supposed to belong to McCoy's band of Missouri robbers."[21] Interestingly, that bit of piracy, which Cole conveniently forgot to mention in his letter, took place in Morehouse Parish, just across the river from Carroll Parish, where he claimed he and Bob were staying.

Assuming Cole's alibi was valid, our suspicions might turn to his brothers Jim and John. It will be recalled that these two turned up together in St. Clair County about the time, or soon after, the retreating train robbers passed through that area. Perhaps Jim and John were the robbers described by a witness as "apparently brothers, being very much alike in form and face."

Cole of course denied the guilt of any of the Youngers, but he did admit that John had returned to Missouri from California in the winter of 1873-74, "just in time to be suspected of the train robbery at Gads Hill."[22] Guilty or not, John paid for the crime when he was killed by Pinkertons in the Roscoe gunfight. As for Jim, authorities suspected him mainly because he was a Younger and, like John, had no alibi.

Cole, Jim, and Bob Younger were captured by a Minnesota posse in September 1876, after the failed Northfield bank raid in which the bank cashier and a pedestrian were killed. While awaiting trial for murder, they were visited in jail by a number of people, including the two Minnesota victims of the Gads Hill robbery, John L. Merriam and John F. Lincoln. The *Minneapolis Tribune* reported:

> Mr. Lincoln is positive Cole Younger was one of the [Gads Hill robbers]. He says he cannot mistake the peculiar shape of the face, and the head which was exposed by his hat falling near Mr. Lincoln's seat [during the robbery], as he gave Mr. Lincoln's own chapeau a revengeful kick. Mr. Merriam is not so certain, but Mr. Lincoln is positive he cannot be wrong. [The] three men wore handkerchiefs over their faces at that time, not, however, over the head and neck.[23]

Cole and Bob separately denied to Merriam and Lincoln that they had anything to do with Gads Hill, but according to the *Faribault Democrat* "their denial was not conclusive." The newspaper stated that each gave a different account of their whereabouts the day the train was robbed, "with a distance of 600 miles between the points."[24] Brother Jim, recovering from a severe bullet wound to the jaw received during his capture, was unable to talk with visitors.

The three Youngers were sentenced to life in the Minnesota State Penitentiary for the Northfield crime. In July 1889, friends and family met with the Minnesota governor in an effort to get the men pardoned. A special plea was presented by their sister, Henrietta, to at least release Bob, who was by then suffering from consumption and was near death. Ironically, the governor at that time was William R. Merriam, son of Gads Hill victim John L. Merriam. This fact obviously influenced his decision, because after hearing all arguments, he arose from his chair and stated, "I cannot pardon these men. My duty to the state and my personal prejudice against them make it impossible."[25] Bob Younger died two months later, September 16, 1889. He was six weeks shy of his thirty-sixth birthday.

On July 10, 1901, after serving twenty-five years in prison, Cole and Jim were released. Under the terms of their pardon they were not allowed to leave Minnesota. The brothers found menial employment and lived as honorably as they could. Fifteen months later, Jim Younger was found dead in his hotel room of a self-inflicted gunshot wound.

Eventually, restrictions were lifted, and in February 1903 Cole was allowed to return home to Missouri. He spent the remainder of his life lecturing on the evils of crime and for a few years toured with Frank James in a Wild West show known as "The Great Cole Younger and Frank James Historical Wild West."

On August 21, 1913, at a tent revival in Lee's Summit, Missouri, Cole Younger responded to the evangelist's invitation to come forward and repent. One hundred fifty-one people were saved that night, Cole among them. He was baptized and joined the Christian Church of Lee's Summit.[26]

Cole died March 21, 1916, at the age of seventy-two and was buried beside his mother and brothers Jim and Bob, in the Lee's Summit Cemetery. John's body remained in the Yeater Cemetery in St. Clair County.

The James Brothers

And 'twas in the county Wayne
That they robbed the Gads Hill train—
Those outlaw brothers Frank and Jesse James.

Including their time as Confederate guerrillas during the Civil War and their bandit activities after, Frank and Jesse James survived as hunted men for nearly two decades. Among the many crimes laid at their door was the train robbery at Gads Hill. As time passed and more and more circumstantial evidence came to light, their guilt became virtually certain.

Jesse Woodson James, generally considered leader of the gang, was born September 5, 1847, near Centerville, Missouri—later renamed Kearney. At maturity he stood five feet eight inches tall and weighed about 165 pounds.[27] His eyes, which blinked constantly, were large and pale blue; his nose, short and slightly upturned. He kept his sandy brown beard neatly trimmed and somewhat short; in later years his hair was usually dyed black. Two bullet wounds badly scarred the right side of his chest—one received during the war, the other in a skirmish with Federal troops soon after the war ended. The tip of his middle finger, left hand, was missing; some say it had been accidentally shot off by Jesse himself. Later in his outlaw career he would also suffer a leg wound.

According to former gang member Dick Liddil, Jesse was a graceful rider and sat very erect in the saddle. When on foot he walked with straight posture and stepped quickly. He was also noticeably bow-legged.

When not robbing banks and trains, the outlaw chief dressed tastefully, usually wearing gloves and a derby. He even occasionally sported a top hat, despite the fact that he claimed to despise the rich gentlemen who wore them. On a raid, said Liddil, Jesse dressed very common, typically wearing a "dark calico shirt and ducking overalls, [with] pants in boots."[28]

Alexander Franklin James, born in Clay County, Missouri, January 10, 1843, looked not at all like Jesse. This older brother was five feet ten inches tall and quite thin, never weighing more than 145 pounds his entire life.[29] His posture was slightly stooped, and he walked, according to Liddil, "like a string-halted horse."[30] His eyes were gray and deep-set, his nose and ears prominent. He had an adequate crop of brown hair at the time of the Gads Hill robbery and often wore "burnside" whiskers. Frank had a penchant for dark clothing. He sometimes wore a long coat and, like brother Jesse, fancied top hat or derby head-gear. On a raid he usually wore a black slouch hat.

Frank and Jesse were quite different in personality as well. Jesse was a talker. He loved to joke, was outgoing, and made friends easily; but at the same time he was quick-tempered, often acted impulsively, and tended to hold a grudge. Frank, by contrast, was a serious man, quiet, reserved, and scholarly. He enjoyed reading classical literature, Shakespeare in particular. While Jesse professed born-again religion, Frank considered himself a religious agnostic. Both were dangerous men in a tight situation.

Did Jesse James rob the train at Gads Hill? Yes, according to his widow, Zee James, in an 1882 newspaper interview two weeks after Jesse's death. The amount taken during the robbery was about two thousand dollars, she claimed, and Jesse's share was one-fifth. With that money the two married and went to Sherman, Texas, on their honeymoon.[31] Frank James married later the same year.

Although Zee freely admitted to her husband's part in the Gads Hill affair, she said he had nothing to do with the stage holdup at Hot Springs. Evidence suggested otherwise, of course. Not only had the stage robbers' trail led from Hot Springs to Gads Hill, but the gold watch stolen from stage passenger John A. Burbank was found in Jesse's possession after his death.[32]

Following Gads Hill, the James brothers continued in the robbery business for eight more years. Then, on April 3, 1882, at his home in St. Joseph, Missouri, Jesse made a fatal mistake. While in the living room with new gang members Robert and Charles Ford, the fabled outlaw removed his pistols and stood on a chair to dust a wall picture. Young Bob Ford, his thoughts on reward money and recognition, shot his unarmed leader in the back of the head.

Jesse James, dead at thirty-four, was survived by his wife and two small children—a seven-year-old son, Jesse Edwards James, and a three-year-old daughter, Mary. He was buried beneath a coffee bean tree in the backyard of the old homeplace near Kearney. When Zee died in 1900, the outlaw's remains were removed and laid to rest beside hers in Mt. Olivet Cemetery in Kearney.

On October 5, six months after Jesse's death, Frank James, tired of running from the law and fearing perhaps a fate similar to his brother's, walked into the state capitol building in Jefferson City and by prearrangement surrendered his pistols to the governor of Missouri. Frank stood trial twice and was acquitted each time.[33] He lived the rest of his days as a law-abiding citizen and died at the James farm February 18, 1915, at age seventy-two. He was survived by his wife, Annie, and a grown son, Robert. At Frank's request there were no religious services performed at his funeral.[34] The old outlaw was cremated, and his ashes were kept in a bank vault until Annie's death, July 6, 1944. At that time their remains were buried together in Hill Park Cemetery, Independence, Missouri.

In 1995 the bones of Jesse James were dug up again, this time for DNA analysis to prove that the body buried in Kearney was indeed that of the famous outlaw. Forensic scientists confirmed what most of us already knew—it was. They "laid poor Jesse in his grave" one final time, October 28, 1995.

In 1874 there was little doubt that Frank and Jesse James were among the robbers at Gads Hill, and nothing has surfaced since to change that belief. Jesse's widow admitted to Jesse's part, and it was surely Frank who quoted those lines of Shakespeare on the train that evening. The identities of their accomplices, however, still remain open to question. Some insist that Cole Younger helped with the holdup; others believe that he and his brother Bob were in Louisiana or Arkansas at the time. Perhaps Jim Younger and Clell Miller participated; many writers seem to think so. And John Younger certainly should not be overlooked as a suspect; nor should gang member Arthur McCoy, whose "death" prior to the robbery was never proven.

So, who robbed the Gads Hill train? At best we can only speculate. This question, like so many involving the Missouri outlaws, will never be fully answered and must forever remain part of the mystique, romance, and legend of Jesse James. And, frankly, this writer would not have it any other way.

CHAPTER 20

Gads Hill—a Final Visit

I beheld, and lo, there was no man, and
all the birds of the heavens were fled.

—Jer. 4:25

Seven miles north of Piedmont, Missouri, on Highway 49, lies the ghost that was once Gads Hill. Described by conductor Chauncey Alford in 1874 as "a small place, of no account," the former settlement is today even smaller and more no account than it was back then. No one lives there anymore. No one wants to. Were it not for a "city limit" sign, a country tavern, and a historical marker, the place would not exist at all. The marker reads: "GADS HILL TRAIN ROBBERY. JESSE JAMES WITH FOUR MEMBERS OF HIS BAND CARRIED OUT THE FIRST MISSOURI TRAIN ROBBERY HERE, JANUARY 31, 1874."

Jesse and his gang may have indeed raided Gads Hill in 1874, but the village has since been robbed of much more and by the greatest thief of them all—Father Time. The original shanties and store building seen by the outlaws have long ago decayed into dust. Gone, too, are the railroad platform, sidetrack, and, of course, the famous old tree "where Jesse tied his horse." Even the wagon road that led east to Peach Tree—by which the gang allegedly entered Gads Hill—is now but a faint impression, barely visible in the undergrowth south of the tavern. The old road was still in use until the mid-1970s, when strip-mining operations forced its closure.

In the 1940s the Iron Mountain tracks (then Missouri Pacific) were removed and rerouted several yards east. Trains, today towed by high-powered Union Pacific diesels, still roar past Gads Hill as did their smaller, steam-driven ancestors, but they no longer stop.[1] Traces of the old road bed, void of rails and cross-ties and with stunted trees growing from its surface, can still be found just north in the nearby woods. It appears now simply as a crude earthen mound running a straight, narrow, slightly downhill course through the scrub timber. While portions of the road bed can be seen intermittently in fields and woods along Highway 49, here it has special significance. This particular section was the well-known grade the Little Rock Express ascended that cold winter evening, just moments before being boarded and robbed by Jesse James.

An Ozark mountain once stood across the Union Pacific tracks behind the village, but like the vast pine forest, it too has fallen victim to progress. Today, a large rhyolite quarry occupies the spot. That ancient hill, which was once a proud part of the landscape, has now been reduced to giant gravel piles and is gradually being hauled away by truck and train to other parts of the country. "Jesse James was small potatoes," a grinning mine employee once told me. "He only stole money from Gads Hill; we took a whole mountain!"

When Jesse robbed the train, only about fifteen people lived at Gads Hill, but the village later prospered as new sawmills opened. By 1889 its population had grown to 320 and during the lumber boom is said to have reached 600. At one time it boasted three steam sawmills, a water-powered flour mill, a hotel, a blacksmith shop, and a railroad depot.[2] After the virgin pine was harvested from the region, people began to move away, and by the mid-1940s old Gads Hill had virtually ceased to be. About all that remains now are a few crumbling concrete foundations of those latter-day dwellings.

Although the old village perished with time, it was not completely forgotten. In the autumn of 1948, nearly seventy-five years after the robbery, a rumor spread that a man cutting wood near Gads Hill had discovered some train loot hidden in a cave—$100,000, it was said! Understandably, the story caused quite a stir. Big-city news reporters quickly descended on Wayne County, and two agents of the United States Treasury Department were sent down from Washington, D.C., to investigate the matter. The excitement faded as quickly as it began, however, when it was learned that the man had in fact found only a few old coins, a moldering book, and a rusty muzzleloading rifle—none of which was connected to Jesse James nor the train robbery. The exaggeration, so stated the *St. Louis Globe-Democrat,* "was merely the workings of normal backyard gossip."

On June 9, 1960, the marker designating the site of Missouri's first train robbery was erected by the Piedmont Lions Club. With that last gasp of publicity, peace and quiet returned once again to Gads Hill—and so it has remained these many years.

Gads Hill today. The rhyolite quarry, in the left background, looms above the Jesse James Saloon. At far right is the sign marking the robbery site.

As I stand at Gads Hill today in solitude, reflecting, my research completed and book written, I recall the eyewitness accounts of the drama that took place here so long ago. For a few moments the past comes alive again, if only in my imagination. The Little Rock Express screeches to a halt as it did back in 1874 and Jesse, Frank, and the Youngers take command. Shouts of "Go back into the cars!" "Keep your seats!" "We'll shoot the first man that stirs!" "Dish out, or be shot!" are heard again as villagers cower close to the bonfire. Little Ami Dean, his face streaked with dried tears, is hiding behind his mother's skirt. Billy and Mr. Farris are standing nearby talking with the masked guard. Aboard the train a waggish outlaw opens the express messenger's receipt book and writes, "Robbed at Gads Hill." A six-year-old boy asks, "Ma, where are the police?" Frank James spouts a few lines of Shakespeare to his captive audience. There are many other sights and sounds from the past—then noise from a passing car rudely interrupts the fantasy, and my thoughts quickly tumble back into the present century.

As I turn to go, my toe strikes a hard metal object partially buried in the dirt of the old road bed. I stoop, brush back the leaves, and pull from its nineteenth-century grave a badly corroded railroad spike, one obviously overlooked by workmen when they removed the Iron Mountain rails decades ago. Although it is only a piece of rusty iron, I am glad to have found it. The spike is, after all, a relic of the original Gads Hill and was there as a silent witness when Jesse James and his notorious outlaw band committed Missouri's first train robbery. It will be preserved and kept as a remembrance of that historic event.

A short time later, back at the robbery site, I climb into my truck and toss the old railroad spike onto the floorboard. The sun is riding low in the west, a gentle autumn breeze stirs the branches of a nearby oak, and high in the sky a flock of crows fly over on their way to roost. My thoughts turn one last time to the Gads Hill of long ago, to Frank and Jesse James, conductor Alford, Rev. T. H. Hagerty, Tom Fitz, "Uncle Jimmy" Sutterfield, and the many other people and places I have come to know during my years of research. I sit for awhile recalling them fondly. Then, bidding farewell to the past, I start the engine and slowly drive away.

Notes

Introduction

1. *Kansas City Times,* September 27, 1872. Some news accounts said the girl was stepped on by a horse. Thirteen years after being shot at by Jesse James and his gang, the cashier, Ben Wallace, was blessed with the birth of a granddaughter, Bess. Bess Wallace would one day be First Lady of the United States, as the wife of Pres. Harry S. Truman. (See Yeatman, 103, 104.)

2. *St. Joseph (Missouri) Morning Herald,* July 27, 1873. (See Settle, 47, 48.)

3. During the war, Maj. John Newman Edwards served as adjutant to Confederate general Joseph O. Shelby. In November 1873, as editor of the *St. Louis Dispatch,* he wrote and published a lengthy article entitled "A Terrible Quintette," which focused on the histories, persecutions, war heroics, and alleged innocence of Arthur McCoy, Frank and Jesse James, and Cole and John Younger. Years later he would help arrange the surrender of Frank James and support the outlaw through two court trials.

Chapter 1

1. The Cairo and Fulton was part of the St. Louis and Iron Mountain Railway system. The two roads joined a few miles below the Arkansas-Missouri border, forming a rail line from St. Louis to Little Rock and southwest into Texas.

2. The stagecoach was robbed about three miles west of Arcadia, Louisiana, January 8, 1874. Afterward, the retreating bandits were seen near the Arkansas border, fourteen miles north of Homer, Louisiana, riding hard in the general direction of Arkadelphia. (*New Orleans Republican,* reprinted in the *Little Rock Arkansas Gazette,* February 7, 1874.)

3. The stories of Easley and Price are from the *Little Rock Republican,* January 20, 1874.

4. See Steele with Warfel, 40, 41.

5. Dacus, 161, 162.

6. *Little Rock Arkansas Gazette,* January 18, 1874. Mr. Crump, whose eyewitness account was the source for much of this chapter, told his story to the *Gazette* upon arriving in Little Rock Saturday night, two days after the holdup.

7. Ibid.

8. Ibid.

9. See Settle, 118. The *Kansas City Times* (reprinted in the *Boonville [Missouri] Weekly Advertiser,* April 28, 1882) described Burbank's recovered property as "an eighteen-karat gold watch, stem-winder, with hunting case, made by Charles J. E. Jaeat; case No. 8289; movement No. 8389." The case, attached to "a heavy eighteen-karat gold chain," was monogrammed "T. A. B."

Chapter 2

1. *Little Rock Republican,* January 20, 1874.

2. Ibid.

3. Ibid. This was a telegram sent by Gillis to a Col. E. A. Nickels soon after the plundered stage arrived at Hot Springs. Other than their names, neither man was identified.

4. *Little Rock Republican,* January 30, 1874, and *Pocahontas (Arkansas) Weekly Observer,* February 10, 1874.

5. *Little Rock Arkansas Gazette,* February 4, 1874.

6. *Little Rock Arkansas Gazette* (reprinted in the *St. Louis Republican,* February 6, 1874). Chalk Bluff Road (formerly the Old Shawnee Trail) followed the high ground of Crowley's Ridge, which extends up through eastern Arkansas and into southeastern Missouri.

7. Moark, Arkansas, located on the state line roughly halfway between Little Rock and St. Louis, was the turnaround point for Missouri and Arkansas train crews. St. Louis trainmen would run southbound trains from St. Louis to the state line, spend the night in Moark, and return home the next day on the northbound. Little Rock crews did likewise in the other direction.

8. In 1874, Poplar Bluff, Missouri, the seat of Butler County, had a population of about a thousand. The story of the James boys stopping for "lunch" appeared in Poplar Bluff's newspaper, the *Daily American Republic,* August 22, 1949. If the incident did occur, the paper erred in stating that the visit was made "the day after" the Gads Hill train was robbed.

9. Jack Myers told me the basic story in 1997 as he had heard it from his grandmother. Cheryl Oberhaus, Jack's cousin, furnished other details from family records. John L. Miller later moved his family to Texas and then to Oklahoma. He had other children with his second wife. In all he was married six times. His third wife, Margaret, died of rabies. John L. passed away in 1915 at age eighty-six; daughter Massie (who was given the dime) died in 1953 at almost eighty-five.

10. *St. Louis Times,* February 1, 1874. The McFadden clan (formerly McFaddin) was well represented in the Mill Spring area in 1874, and some of its descendants still live there today. One of the boys, Adolphus Bernard McFadden, six years old when Jesse James visited the village, later changed his name to Bernarr Macfadden, moved away, and went on to worldwide fame and fortune as a physical-fitness guru, lecturer, writer, and publisher. In the 1940s and 1950s, the eccentric Macfadden, then in his eighties, enjoyed making headlines by leaping over chairs, standing on his head for fifteen minutes at a time, parachuting out of airplanes, and doing other physically demanding stunts. He claimed that his special vegetarian diet and exercise program would retard the aging process and enable him to live to 125. He died of jaundice, October 12, 1955, at the tender age of eighty-seven. Among the magazines still published by the company he founded are *True Confessions, True Story, True Romance,* and others of that genre.

11. The outlaws' ride through Piedmont and their stop at Widow Gilbreath's is from the *St. Louis Republican,* February 2, 1874.

Chapter 3

1. Plum Street Station stood near the Mississippi River in St. Louis at (what was then) Fourth and Plum, in the vicinity of present-day Poplar Street Bridge.

2. According to the *1874 Iron Mountain Railway Annual Report,* about two-thirds of the company's locomotives were still wood-burners; one-third had been altered to burn coal.

3. Contemporary newspapers generally gave the conductor's name as C. A. Alford, but he was also mentioned as C. W. Alford and C. H. Alford. Various St. Louis city directories listed him as C. H. Alford, Chauncy H. Alford, and Chauncey H. Alford (with an *e*). According to family records his middle name was Higley.

4. At age twenty-nine James H. Morley had been assigned the monumental task of running a rail line from St. Louis to the rich ore-mining region of the southeastern Missouri Ozarks, an area that for years had been mined by the French. The line was to terminate somewhere in the vicinity of Iron Mountain, for which the railroad was named. Morley chose the nearby village of Pilot Knob as its temporary terminus. After the Civil War another engineer was put in charge, and construction resumed. On October 10, 1871, the road from Pilot Knob south into Arkansas, known as the Iron Mountain Extension, was opened for travel. (See Walker, "A Brief History.")

5. September 27, 1864, at Pilot Knob, Missouri, in the gap between Pilot Knob Mountain and Shepherd Mountain, Gen. Sterling Price and several thousand Confederates attacked Fort Davidson, a Federal garrison commanded by Gen. Thomas Ewing. Despite being heavily outnumbered, the Federal troops inflicted more than a thousand casualties on their attackers while losing fewer than a hundred themselves.

Chapter 4

1. Gad's Hill, England, was an old agricultural village in north Kent, three miles northwest of Rochester.

2. *Little Rock Republican,* February 17, 1874. Hoop poles were dried hickory strips that coopers wrapped around large barrels (hogsheads) to secure the staves.

3. Conductor Chauncey Alford, *St. Louis Times,* February 2, 1874; see also Campbell, *Campbell's Gazetteer,* 639.

4. *St. Louis Republican,* February 2, 1874. In one interview conductor Alford referred to Gads Hill as "a regular stopping-place"; in another he was quoted as saying, "We always stop at Gads Hill." Perhaps Alford was calling the slowdown for mail exchange a "stop."

5. This story was told by Coker Montgomery during a tape-recorded interview with his nephew, Norrid Montgomery, in 1974. Coker passed away at age seventy-nine, a year after the recording was made.

Chapter 5

1. Thomas Purrington Fitz enlisted at Charlottesville, Virginia, June 18, 1861, in Company H, First Virginia Artillery. Later, with permission from his commanding officers, he traded places with a J. L. Shop and served out the rest of the war in Company I, Fifth Virginia Cavalry. His favorite expression, I'm told, was "Gae God almighty!" Considering all the dangers he experienced during his lifetime, Tom must have uttered the phrase many times. In later years he owned a store in Des Arc and enjoyed handing out mints to neighborhood children. Tom Fitz died January 6, 1927, at age eighty-six. His wife, Alice, died five days later. They are buried at Mountain View Cemetery, Des Arc, Missouri. (Information received from Alice White and Jeanette Parker, granddaughter and great-granddaughter of Tom Fitz.)

2. Masnor. The article was the substance of an interview with a Dave Miller, whose family had taken care of Billy Farris in his waning years.

3. These descriptions were later given by Alford, Hagerty, and other men aboard the train.

4. The story of Dean's meeting with the robbers was told to me by Carl Laxton, who said he heard it from Dean in the late 1930s or early 1940s. Carl said that at that time Dean was an avid gardener, and he enjoyed growing his own pipe tobacco.

5. *St. Louis Republican,* February 2, 1874. According to Cramer (239), the storekeeper's name was Walter Zeitinger, and she wrote that he and Tom Fitz were tied up by the robbers. Contemporary newspapers, however, gave the storekeeper's name as McMillen and made no mention of anyone being tied up.

6. *Goodspeed's History,* 629.

Chapter 6

1. The quotes from conductor Alford regarding his initial encounter with the outlaws are from the *St. Louis Times, St. Louis Globe,* and *St. Louis Republican,* February 2, 1874, and the *Chicago Tribune,* February 4, 1874.

2. Hagerty told his story in a letter to the editor, which appeared in the *St. Louis Globe,* February 4, 1874.

3. *St. Louis Dispatch,* February 5, 1874.

4. *St. Louis Democrat,* February 11, 1874 (from a reporter's interview with State Rep. L. M. Farris upon his returning to his office in Jefferson City a few days after the robbery).

5. Masnor.

6. *Little Rock Republican,* February 4, 1874. News reporters in 1874 invariably misspelled the name of the Missouri village, "Gad's Hill" (with an apostrophe). To avoid confusion I took the liberty of correcting the spelling to "Gads Hill" (without an apostrophe) in this and all other quotes and excerpts throughout the book.

7. Express messenger Wilson, *St. Louis Dispatch,* February 5, 1874.

8. *St. Louis Times,* February 2, 1874. This was told to conductor Alford by residents on his return trip through Gads Hill the next day.

Chapter 7

1. Conductor Chauncey Alford, *St. Louis Globe,* February 2, 1874.

2. *St. Louis Dispatch,* February 5, 1874.

3. Ibid.

4. *St. Louis Globe,* February 2, 1874.

5. As quoted by Wilson, *St. Louis Dispatch,* February 5, 1874.

6. *St. Louis Democrat,* February 4, 1874.

Chapter 8

1. *St. Louis Democrat,* February 4, 1874. ("Plug hat" was another name for a top hat, usually made of silk or beaver fur.) The *Arkadelphia (Arkansas) Ouachita Commercial* facetiously commented: "We advise all travelers hereafter to leave their 'plug' or 'stove-pipe' hats at home, or throw them out of the window before they get into the woods."

2. *Little Rock Republican,* February 13, 1874. This contradicted a statement made by conductor Alford that no one in the smoking car was robbed.

3. *St. Louis Democrat,* February 4, 1874.

4. *St. Louis Globe,* February 4, 1874.

5. Henry, *St. Louis Times,* February 2, 1874.

6. *St. Louis Globe, February 4, 1874.* As most readers of outlaw history know, the father of Frank and Jesse James had himself been a Baptist minister. Rev. Robert James went West during the gold rush in 1850 to join his brother in

California—some say to do missionary work—and died of fever not long after arriving. Frank was only seven at the time; Jesse was three. One of the many accomplishments of Robert James was helping found Baptist-affiliated William Jewell College (in Liberty, Missouri), a school still going strong today.

7. *Little Rock Republican,* February 4, 1874.

8. Various newspapers spelled the name McClarren, McClann, McLanan, McLain, and McKahn. This passenger, whatever his name or nationality, lived in Memphis and worked as a conductor for the Memphis and Louisville Railroad.

9. *St. Louis Republican,* February 1, 1874. According to conductor Alford's statement to the *St. Louis Times,* they also asked for a detective named Gratwein.

10. America's first armed train robbery was pulled off by the Reno brothers, October 6, 1866, near Seymour, Indiana. Other train robberies followed, courtesy of the Renos and their imitators, but within a couple of years all parties had been caught and punished. Some were sent up for long prison terms; others were hanged by angry lynch mobs.

11. According to a 1907 speech made by William A. Pinkerton (Allan's son), the agency was first hired to hunt the James-Younger outlaws following the robbery of the Ocobock Brothers Bank in Corydon, Iowa, June 3, 1871.

12. *St. Louis Globe,* February 4, 1874.

13. From Shakespeare's *King Henry IV,* Part I, Act I, Scene 2.

14. From Shakespeare's *King Henry VI,* Part I, Act II, Scene 2.

Chapter 9

1. *St. Louis Times,* February 2, 1874.

2. *Arkadelphia (Arkansas) Ouachita Commercial.*

3. *St. Louis Globe-Democrat,* September 28, 1876 (special dispatch to the *Minneapolis Tribune* from Faribault, Minnesota). John Lincoln came to this conclusion after visiting Cole Younger in the Faribault jail.

4. *Little Rock Arkansas Gazette,* February 3, 1874. The reporter may have fudged a bit on this story. In reality, there were no male passengers from New England listed.

5. *St. Louis Republican,* February 2, 1874, and *Little Rock Republican,* February 3, 1874.

6. *St. Louis Republican,* February 2, 1874.

7. News agent Butler, *St. Louis Times,* February 2, 1874.

8. *Little Rock Republican,* February 3, 1874.

9. Ibid., February 4, 1874.

10. *St. Louis Globe,* February 2, 1874.

11. Passenger C. H. Henry, *St. Louis Times,* February 2, 1874.

12. Conductor Chauncey Alford, *St. Louis Globe* and *St. Louis Times,* February 2, 1874. In his statement to the *Times,* Alford said that the robbers blamed the misrepresentation on the *Dispatch's* owner, Stilson Hutchins, and specified that it was in regard to the Hot Springs stage holdup—or, as they called it, "the Malvern Hill affair."

13. *St. Louis Times,* February 1, 1874.

14. *Little Rock Arkansas Gazette,* February 3, 1874. (In its article, the newspaper erroneously gave the *St. Louis Dispatch* owner's name as "Silas Hutchins.")

15. Mark Twain, in chapter 29 of *Life on the Mississippi,* wrote of this man as "Murel." Twain briefly compared Murel's prowess as an outlaw to Jesse James, and in his opinion Jesse came out on the short end.

16. *Little Rock Arkansas Gazette,* February 3, 1874, and October 9, 1966.

Chapter 10

1. *Lexington (Missouri) Weekly Caucasian;* see also Settle, 71. Professor Allen was among a group of passengers aboard an omnibus stopped and robbed by highwaymen, Sunday afternoon, August 30, 1874, just across the Missouri River from Lexington.

2. *St. Louis Globe,* February 4, 1874.

3. *St. Louis Times,* February 2, 1874. Passenger C. H. Henry, clerk at the Clear Water Lumber Company, said he was of the opinion that the robbery was planned "for the purpose of robbing Mr. Staunchfield; and if he and the money had been on the train, no other person or property would have been molested."

4. Zerelda ("Zee") James, *Kansas City Evening Star.*

5. A complete list of the Gads Hill robbery victims and their losses was never published. The following is from partial lists printed in various newspapers. *Passengers:* Mrs. Scott surrendered $400; John Merriam (also written as Meriam and Morran), $200, $360, or $50; John Lincoln, $200 or $50; C. H. Henry (also written as T. D. and C. D. Henry), $154 and change; Silas Ferry (also written as Silas Terry), $7.50, $70.50, $750, or $57; G. L. Dart (also written as G. G. Dent), $30; Col. J. H. Morley, $15; A. J. Merriman, $75; J. H. Pearson, $7; and W. A. McClarren (also written as McClann, McLanan, McLain, and McKahn), $15 cash, a $30 finger ring, and a diamond breast pin valued at $100. *Trainmen:* Conductor Chauncey Alford (written as C. A., C. H., and C. W. Alford) lost $50 or $40; express messenger William Wilson, $41.05; sleeping-car conductor O. S. Newell (also written as O. S. Newall), $20; news agent Alfred Butler (also written as James Butler), $50, $40, or $11; baggage master Louis Constant, $5; and porter James Johnson (also written as James Johnston), $2. Also, one gold watch and four pistols were taken from various individuals, as well as lesser items, such as the lady's three handkerchiefs, the man's hat, and Alford's tobacco.

6. *Arkadelphia (Arkansas) Ouachita Commercial.*

7. The tree (a red oak, some say) was still standing as recently as the 1960s, but just barely. When it did eventually fall, people cut off sections as souvenirs. I once talked with a former Gads Hill area resident who as a boy owned a piece of the old tree. He sold it to a drunk man, he said, for three dollars. The man asked him, "Now exactly where on this limb did Jesse James tie his horse?" The boy pointed out a likely spot and said, "Oh, right about there." Satisfied with that answer, the man staggered off with his prize.

8. *St. Louis Democrat,* February 4, 1874. This newspaper stated, "That they are the same party that robbed the Hot Springs stage there is scarcely any doubt. They talked and acted similarly, jocularly mentioned that occurrence two or three times, and one of the horses in their possession was recognized as the one stolen from the stage team."

9. According to the *Tribune Almanac and Political Register,* January 31 was the eve of a full moon and the sun set at 5:21 P.M.

Chapter 11

1. On Sunday morning, Hagerty conducted his scheduled church meeting and later penned a lengthy letter to the editor of the *St. Louis Globe* detailing his experiences at Gads Hill. He also dashed one off to Rev. W. P. Hammond, a popular fire-and-brimstone revivalist then crusading in St. Louis, requesting that Hammond and his congregation pray for the robbers. That letter was mentioned by Hammond Monday morning during a special prayer service being held, strangely enough, in a house of prostitution at 709 Green Street in St. Louis. According to the *St. Louis Globe* (February 4), Hammond, accompanied by three other ministers and "a number of Christian ladies," was there at the invitation of Madame Stillman and "twenty or thirty fallen women" who stayed at the house. The newspaper reported: "Mr. Hammond stated that he received a letter from Rev. Mr. Haggerty [*sic*], who was on the train recently robbed on the Iron Mountain Road, asking prayer for the robbers who had presented their pistols at his head and threatened his life."

2. Reports of the happenings in Carondelet and De Soto, and the story of the St. Louis and Little Rock train crews being armed, appeared in the *St. Louis Times,* February 2, 1874.

3. Greenville, the seat of Wayne County, was then on the St. Francis River, two miles south of its present location. It was moved in the 1940s after persistent flooding. Benjamin Holmes served Wayne County off and on as sheriff, collector, assessor, and state representative beginning in 1847; he represented the county in the seventeenth and eighteenth sessions of the Missouri General Assembly, 1852 and 1854 respectively. He was also noted for supervising construction of a number of major roads in the region. During the Civil War,

Holmes joined the Confederacy as a private, rose through the ranks, and in August 1863 was commissioned lieutenant colonel in Parson's Twelfth Missouri Infantry Regiment. His unit surrendered at Shreveport, Louisiana, June 8, 1865. After restrictions of Missouri's postwar constitution were lifted, he returned to Wayne County politics. Holmes and his wife, Amelia, had no children. When he died, April 29, 1884, she remarried. Colonel Holmes is buried in the Dixon Cemetery, beside Wesley Chapel, near Hiram, Missouri.

4. *St. Louis Times,* February 2, 1874.

5. *St. Louis Democrat,* February 11, 1874. Accounts varied as to when the Holmes posse left Gads Hill. A special dispatch, wired February 1 from Piedmont to the *St. Louis Republican,* stated: "Early this morning about twenty-five horsemen, well-armed, started from Gads Hill in pursuit. They were strongly reinforced on their route." According to conductor Alford, however, the posse was still forming late Sunday morning when his train passed through on the way back to St. Louis; and a man from Corning, Arkansas, who visited Gads Hill a week later, claimed he was told that the posse didn't leave until Monday morning, thirty-six hours after the robbery.

6. Chauncey Higley Alford (written most often as C. A. Alford in old news accounts) was born April 17, 1835, in Wellsboro, Pennsylvania, and on February 3, 1859, married Mary Elizabeth Chrysup in Hamburg, Illinois. During the Civil War he served as a sergeant in the Union Army, Tenth Missouri Infantry, Company B, K. A month after his discharge in 1864, he and Elizabeth moved from Hamburg to St. Louis. At the time of the Gads Hill robbery, they lived in a rented house in the Carondelet community on Third Street between Olive and Nebraska streets. (Today, Third is Minnesota; Olive and Nebraska are Krauss and Haven.) In 1882 Chauncey and his wife moved to Los Angeles and in 1893 took up residence in Jamestown, North Dakota. The couple divorced, January 30, 1894, and two months later he married Henrietta Amanda Kingsley. Chauncey Alford died in Los Angeles, January 14, 1931, at the ripe old age of ninety-five. He was survived by at least one daughter and by Henrietta, who died October 22, 1933.

Chapter 12

1. Governor Woodson's proclamation was written and dated February 2, 1874. It was issued twelve days later, February 14.

2. *St. Louis Dispatch,* February 10, 1874. This newspaper based its accusations on the testimony of a former St. Louis police officer who claimed he knew the James and Younger brothers on sight and had witnessed them rob the bank at Richmond, Missouri, in 1868. Somehow the *Dispatch* concluded that the Richmond and Gads Hill bandits were one and the same group.

3. The original telegram is pasted in Walter B. Stevens' Scrap Book; see also Settle, 50.

4. See Royce's article for this account. In our interview, he told me he heard the old man tell the story in the mid-1950s while camping with deer hunters in a Wayne County cornfield.

5. Campbell, *Campbell's Atlas*.

6. Masnor.

7. *Salem (Missouri) Success* (reprinted in the *St. Louis Republican*, February 14, 1874).

8. Leona Skelton, granddaughter of Jimmy Sutterfield, told me she had heard a similar story from her cousin, whose mother was living in the house when the outlaws visited. Floyd Sutterfield, great-grandson of Jimmy's brother, said he understood that while the men were there they made no secret of their identities. At the time of the horse trade, Jimmy Sutterfield was thirty-three years old—exactly seven years older than Jesse James. (He was born September 5, 1840; Jesse was born September 5, 1847.) Jimmy served two terms as Reynolds County coroner and one term as judge. He died in 1930, ten days before his ninetieth birthday, and is buried in the West Fork Cemetery about a mile from the old homeplace. The valley where Tom's Creek flows into West Fork is today known as "Sutterfield Hollow." In later years someone added a second story to the old log house, and in 1993 it was moved to Caledonia, Missouri, and restored. Today it serves as an antique and curio shop.

9. *Salem (Missouri) Success*.

10. *St. Louis Republican*, February 11, 1874. The name (misspelled "Carpentersville" in the newspaper) was later changed to "Currant River," with an *a*. In 1875 the post office was discontinued.

11. *Salem (Missouri) Success*.

12. *St. Louis Republican*, February 11, 1874.

13. Thomas Welch came to Shannon County, Missouri, from Tennessee and settled near Welch Cave, where he built the grist mill, operated a small store, and constructed a fish trap above the spring. Tom and his wife had a large family. One of their sons was named after the river, Current River Welch. (See Lewis, 8.)

14. From conversations with Bob Howell and Fern George, lifelong residents of northwestern Shannon County and great-grandchildren of Betsy Howell. See also Lewis, 10, 11. According to census records, George Simeon ("Sims") Howell was twenty-eight years old in 1850, his wife, Elizabeth ("Betsy") Howell, was twenty-two, and they had two small children. It is believed that Sims built the cabin in 1853 or 1854. The widowed Betsy would have been forty-six in 1874 when she allegedly fed Jesse James and his gang. (Information received from Brian Driscoll, Ozark National Scenic Riverways, Van Buren, Missouri.)

15. See Lewis, 11. There are other surviving stories of the James brothers' travels in that area. One is that they rode through Cedargrove and camped

awhile on Barren Fork (pronounced "Barn" Fork). Another is that they once spent a few days at the old Boyd Hotel in Eminence and before leaving town had a horse shod. It is also said they occasionally spent time with friends Jesse and Lizzie Heaton in Mash Hollow.

16. Information obtained from the National Park Service and from visits to Howell's cabin.

17. *Little Rock Republican*, February 6, 1874.

18. *Little Rock Arkansas Gazette*, February 24, 1874.

Chapter 13

1. *St. Louis Republican*, February 11, 1874.

2. *Salem (Missouri) Success* (reprinted in the *St. Louis Republican*, February 14, 1874).

3. *Arkadelphia (Arkansas) Ouachita Commercial.*

4. *Boston Post* (reprinted in the *St. Louis Globe*, February 6, 1874).

5. *St. Louis Republican*, February 11, 1874.

6. Ibid., February 13, 1874. Dexter Mason, born in Vermont (1811), and Laura Parker Mason, born in New York (1810), were married in Massachusetts and eventually settled in Texas County, Missouri. At the outbreak of the Civil War, Dexter and his three eldest sons enlisted in the Union Army. The father and two of his sons later returned home, but the other son died in a St. Louis hospital. In 1875 and 1876 Dexter Mason, a Democrat, represented Texas County in the state legislature. By occupation he was a farmer. Dexter died at age seventy-three; his wife, Laura, at seventy-five. Four sons and two daughters survived. (See *History of Laclede*, 1130.)

7. This crossroad, shown on an 1874 Texas County map, was located in the vicinity of present-day Success, Missouri.

8. *Salem (Missouri) Success*. The newspaper stated that the robbers were "evidently aiming for the South Pacific road near Springfield." That speculation later proved wrong.

9. *St. Louis Republican*, February 11, 1874.

10. *Bolivar (Missouri) Free Press*, February 19, 1874. The day before the Brush Creek sighting, five armed bandits held up a store at Bentonville, Arkansas, dozens of miles to the southwest, and made off with $200 cash and about $100 in merchandise. A couple of days later, forty miles north, thieves took $3,100 from an Adams Express office in Granby City, Missouri. Although it was physically impossible for the Gads Hill robbers to have performed either of those raids, newspapers blamed them nonetheless.

11. See Zink, 6.

Chapter 14

1. *St. Louis Republican*, October 6, 1882, statement by Frank James just prior to his surrender.

2. *St. Louis Dispatch,* February 10, 1874.

3. Ibid., March 16, 1874. Whicher's parents lived in Des Moines, Iowa; his new bride in Iowa City. He was formerly a sailor on an ocean vessel but gave up the sea after falling from the masthead and breaking an ankle. At the time of Whicher's mission in Clay County, Missouri, he had been a detective about three years. (*Chicago Tribune,* March 21, 1874.)

4. *Kansas City Times,* March 14, 1874 (reprinted in the *Liberty [Missouri] Tribune,* March 20, 1874).

5. *St. Louis Globe,* March 20, 1874.

6. Reprinted in the *St. Louis Republican,* March 23, 1874.

7. Ibid.

8. *Kansas City Times,* March 1874 (reprinted in the *St. Louis Dispatch,* March 16, 1874).

9. Chicago Tribune, March 21, 1874.

10. Ibid.

11. *Chicago Tribune,* February 2, 1875.

12. See Younger, 93.

13. *Kansas City Times,* March 1874 (reprinted in the *St. Louis Dispatch,* March 16, 1874).

14. Reprinted in the *St. Louis Republican,* March 23, 1874.

15. Statement by Dick Liddil after his surrender to Sheriff James H. Timberlake January 24, 1882. (See Breihan, *The Man Who Shot Jesse James,* 191.)

16. Local gossip suggested that Clay County's one-armed sheriff, George E. Patton, an old friend of the James boys, had ridden out and forewarned them of Whicher's coming. In an angry letter to the *Liberty (Missouri) Tribune,* March 27, 1874, Patton proclaimed that anyone who made such a statement was "a liar of the 'first water'." He also sued the *St. Louis Globe* and *St. Louis Republican* for printing the gossip, but both suits were later dropped.

17. *Chicago Tribune,* March 21, 1874.

18. *St. Louis Globe,* March 20, 1874.

19. Ibid.

Chapter 15

1. *Chicago Tribune,* March 22, 1874, and *Chicago Times,* May 8, 1874. Louis Lull had been a cadet midshipman at the Naval Academy before resigning to serve in the Union Army in November 1864. He was employed as a hotel detective at the Palmer House in Chicago for three weeks at fifty dollars a month, plus board, prior to hiring on with the Pinkertons.

2. See Appler, 172. Appler, then editor of the *Osceola (Missouri) Democrat,* claimed to have interviewed Boyle.

3. See Brant, 134-35.

Chapter 16

1. Theodrick Snuffer (sometimes written as Theodoric) was born July 15, 1799, in Virginia. He and his wife, Margaret, came to St. Clair County, Missouri, in 1838, where they settled and raised a family. (See *History of Henry & St. Clair Counties,* 1149, 1150.)

2. See Appler, 174.

3. *St. Louis Globe,* April 3, 1874.

4. Quoted by a *Chicago Inter-Ocean* reporter who interviewed the wounded Detective Allen in Roscoe.

5. *St. Louis Dispatch,* March 21, 1874.

6. Coroner's inquest.

7. Ibid.

8. *Bolivar (Missouri) Free Press,* March 26, 1874.

9. Coroner's inquest. The pistol McDonald received from Jim Younger was described as an army-sized Remington that had evidently seen much service. The name *Soule* was neatly carved in the wooden grip. (*St. Louis Times,* March 24, 1874.)

10. *Bolivar (Missouri) Free Press,* March 26, 1874.

11. Verdict of the coroner's jury, March 18, 1874.

Chapter 17

1. Attending physician Dr. D. C. McNeill said the one-ounce ball "went clean through him, entering about two inches and a half below the left nipple, passing through the lower lobe of the lung, and coming out under the seventh rib."

2. *Bolivar (Missouri) Free Press,* March 26, 1874. According to the *St. Louis Globe,* April 3, 1874: "When the negroes found him he feigned dead, and he distinctly heard some one call out, 'kill him'—he supposes it to have been Jim Younger—but the darkies lifted him up and carried him to their cabin."

3. See Zink, 17.

4. *St. Louis Dispatch,* March 21, 1874 (special correspondence from Clinton, Missouri).

5. See Zink, 21, 22.

6. *Chicago Times,* May 8, 1874. This newspaper reported that the detective and his wife, the former Miss May Power, were married August 6, 1873. It stated that ever since his wounding she had watched over him with "jealous care." Armed with a revolver, she vowed that "no person could enter her husband's room to do him harm until they had walked over her dead body." (Another account gave her name as Marian.)

7. Ibid.

8. See Zink, 19.

9. *St. Louis Globe,* March 22, 1874 (special correspondence from Osceola, Missouri).

10. *St. Louis Globe,* April 3, 1874 (correspondence from the *Chicago Inter-Ocean*).

11. *St. Louis Dispatch,* March 24, 1874.

12. *Chicago Times,* March 23, 1874. William Pinkerton and his brother, Robert, would one day inherit the Pinkerton National Detective Agency from their father, Allan.

13. *St. Louis Dispatch,* April 7, 1874.

14. See Yeatman, 120.

15. This letter is on file at the State Historical Society of Missouri, Columbia. (See Horan, 51.)

Chapter 18

1. Letter sent by Allan Pinkerton, April 12, 1874, to George H. Bangs, superintendent of the Pinkerton Agency, New York City. (See Morn, 78, 79.)

2. See Settle, 108. Settle cites the *Kansas City Daily Journal,* July 19, 1881, and the *Richmond (Missouri) Conservator,* July 22, 1881.

Chapter 19

1. Among the early Gads Hill suspects was a thieving gang of ex-Confederates from the Mill Spring area known as the "Ghosts of Shiloh." That group, according to the *St. Louis Times,* consisted of "a dozen adventuresome country loafers who have perpetrated several outrages upon citizens of Wayne, Butler and Carter counties." The *St. Louis Globe* pointed to a similar band of ne'er-do-wells who hung out near the Arkansas border.

2. *St. Louis Dispatch,* February 10, 1874.

3. William Pinkerton, speaking in 1907 at the annual convention of the International Association of Chiefs of Police in Jamestown, Virginia, claimed that the Gads Hill robbers were the James brothers, Younger brothers, Clell Miller, and Jim Cummings (*sic*).

4. *St. Louis Republican,* March 23, 1872. During a saloon quarrel in Pinckneyville, Illinois, Sam Hildebrand, using the alias John Smith, attempted to slash the throat of a bartender and was taken into custody by law officers. Brought immediately before the judge, Sam was found guilty and fined for public drunkenness. A few hours later, as the officers were conveying him to the chambers of a second judge to face the more serious charge of "assault with a deadly weapon," the old war-horse resisted violently. Drawing a concealed knife, he slashed Constable Ragland's thigh open "from knee to the hip." It was Sam Hildebrand's last sinful act; Ragland drew a pistol and shot him dead.

5. A modern flat tombstone has since replaced the original, which I'm told was stolen. It reads: "SAMUEL S. HILDEBRAND / MAJ MO BUSHWHACKER / CONFEDERATE STATES ARMY / JANUARY 6, 1836 - MARCH 21, 1872." (Copied at the gravesite in Park Hills [formerly Elvins], Missouri.)

6. From an old newspaper clipping, St. Louis Public Library (newspaper, title, and date unknown). The article quoted Cummins as saying: "I could ride at a gallop and pick up my hat from the ground, and I didn't need any stirrups, either, in doing that."

7. Statement by Dick Liddil after his surrender to Sheriff James H. Timberlake January 24, 1882. (See Breihan, *The Man Who Shot Jesse James,* 191.)

8. See McCorkle, 114, 115. On one occasion, according to McCorkle, Greenwood's horse was shot from under him during a skirmish. As Bill regained his feet, he found himself facing a mounted Federal soldier who was pointing a pistol and demanding his surrender. "All right," said Bill; then with lightning speed he drew his own pistol and shot the Federal dead. Grabbing the reins of the enemy's horse, he mounted and coolly galloped back to his companions. "Boys," he reportedly said, "I made a good horse trade."

9. See Edwards, *Noted Guerrillas,* 460.

10. It is believed that Clell Miller first rode with the gang June 3, 1871, during the robbery of the Ocobock Brothers Bank at Corydon, Iowa.

11. See Edwards, *Noted Guerrillas,* 316, 317.

12. Ibid., 316.

13. *St. Louis Democrat,* April 11, 1874, and *Liberty (Missouri) Tribune,* April 7, 1874. The account of McCoy's shooting death supposedly came from a man who lived near the Arkansas-Missouri border. McCoy was buried where he fell, it was claimed, and Frank James suffered a shoulder wound but escaped with the others.

14. *St. Louis Dispatch,* April 14, 1874. The account of McCoy's death from consumption came in an unsigned letter from Texas. Its truthfulness was presumed, although never proven.

15. See Merle J. McCoy.

16. *Denison (Texas) News* and *Dallas (Texas) Commercial.* (See Shirley, 119, 120.)

17. *Patterson (Missouri) Times* (article datelined Sherman, Texas, August 16, 1874).

18. When Cole Younger entered prison at age thirty-two, November 20, 1876, he was recorded as being five feet eleven and one-half inches tall and weighing 230 pounds. (According to Croy, 158.)

19. *Pleasant Hill (Missouri) Review.*

20. Dated August 7, 1875, this letter was in reply to one sent by Appler. (See Appler, 49, 50.)

21. *New York Times,* February 4, 1874. The February 3 *New Orleans Picayune* stated, "It is supposed by some that they are a fragment of the famous Coy [*sic*] band of Missouri robbers."

22. See Younger, 68.

23. Reprinted in the *St. Louis Globe-Democrat,* September 28, 1876.

24. *Faribault (Minnesota) Democrat,* September 29, 1876.

25. See Bronaugh, 130. Bronaugh attended the parole hearing.

26. *St. Clair County (Missouri) Democrat.* (See Brant, *The Outlaw Youngers,* 309, 310.)

27. See Rhodes. Rhodes interviewed Frank James at Hot Springs, Arkansas, in 1912.

28. Statement by Dick Liddil after his surrender to Sheriff James H. Timberlake January 24, 1882. (See Miller, 331.)

29. See Rhodes. At his trial, Frank gave his weight as 140 pounds.

30. Statement by Dick Liddil after his surrender to Sheriff James H. Timberlake January 24, 1882.

31. *Kansas City Evening Star.*

32. See Settle, 118.

33. Frank James stood trial for the murder of conductor William Westfall, who was killed during the Winston, Missouri, train robbery, July 15, 1881; he was later also tried for the holdup of a government paymaster in Muscle Shoals, Alabama, which occurred March 11, 1881.

34. *Oklahoma City Daily Oklahoman.* Former federal judge John F. Philips, who defended Frank at his murder trial in Gallatin, Missouri, delivered the funeral address.

Chapter 20

1. When Jesse James robbed the train in January 1874, the railroad was the St. Louis and Iron Mountain. May 6 of that year the company reorganized as the St. Louis, Iron Mountain and Southern. On March 5, 1917, it merged into the Missouri Pacific. It bore that name until purchased by Union Pacific in December 1982.

2. See Cramer, 314. For several years, beginning May 14, 1887, the village was called Zeitonia (after resident and former postmaster Anthony Zeitinger). On April 2, 1906, it was renamed Gads Hill.

Bibliography

Books

Appler, Augustus C. *The Younger Brothers: Their Life and Character.* 1875. Reprint, New York: Frederick Fell, 1955.

Bell, James E. *History of Early Reynolds County, Missouri.* Paducah, Ky: Turner, 1986.

Brant, Marley. *The Outlaw Youngers: A Confederate Brotherhood.* Lanham, Md.: Madison Books, 1992.

Breihan, Carl W. *The Man Who Shot Jesse James.* New York: A. S. Barnes, 1979.

———. *Saga of Jesse James.* Caldwell, Idaho: The Caxton Printers, 1991.

Bronaugh, Warren C. *The Youngers' Fight for Freedom.* Columbia, Mo.: E. W. Stephens, 1906.

Campbell, R. A. *Campbell's Atlas of Missouri.* St. Louis: R. A. Campbell, 1874.

———. *Campbell's Gazeteer of Missouri.* St. Louis: R. A. Campbell, 1874.

Cramer, Rose Fulton. *Wayne County, Missouri.* Cape Girardeau, Mo.: Ramfre Press, 1972.

Crittenden, Henry Hutson, comp. *The Crittenden Memoirs.* New York: G. P. Putnam's Sons, 1936.

Croy, Homer. *Last of the Great Outlaws.* New York: Duell, Sloan and Pearce, 1956.

Cummins, James Robert. *Jim Cummins' Book, Written by Himself.* Denver: Reed, 1903.

Dacus, Joseph A. *Illustrated Lives and Adventures of Frank and Jesse James and the Younger Brothers, the Noted Western Outlaws.* 2nd ed. St. Louis: N. D. Thompson and Company, 1881.

Daniel, Albion and Velma. *Story of Piedmont.* Piedmont, Mo.: Stivers and Ellinghouse, 1955.

Edwards, John Newman. *Noted Guerrillas, or the Warfare of the Border.* St. Louis: Bryan and Company, 1877.

Goodspeed's History of Southeast Missouri. Cape Girardeau, Mo.: Goodspeed, 1888.

History of Henry & St. Clair Counties, Missouri. St. Joseph, Mo.: National Historical, 1883.

History of Laclede, Camden, Dallas, Webster, Wright, Texas, Pulaski, Phelps, and Dent Counties, Missouri. Chicago: Goodspeed, 1889.

Horan, James D. *The Outlaws.* New York: Random House, 1977.

James, Jesse Edwards. *Jesse James, My Father.* Independence, Mo.: Sentinel, 1889.

Lewis, David. *The Current River and Tributaries.* Eminence, Mo.: Ozark, 1978.

Love, Robertus A. *The Rise and Fall of Jesse James.* New York: G. P. Putnam's Sons, 1926.

McCorkle, John. *Three Years with Quantrill: A True Story Told by His Scout, John McCorkle.* 1914. Reprint, Norman, Okla.: University of Oklahoma Press, 1992.

Miller, George, Jr. *The Trial of Frank James for Murder.* Columbia, Mo.: E. W. Stephens, 1898.

Morn, Frank. *The Eye That Never Sleeps: A History of the Pinkerton National Detective Agency.* Bloomington, Ind.: Indiana University Press, 1982.

Reynolds County, Missouri: 1845-1987 Biographical Sketches. Paducah, Ky.: Reynolds County Historical Society, 1987.

Settle, William A., Jr. *Jesse James Was His Name.* Columbia, Mo.: University of Missouri Press, 1966.

Shirley, Glenn. *Belle Starr and Her Times.* Norman, Okla.: University of Oklahoma Press, 1982.

Steele, Phillip W. *Starr Tracks: Belle and Pearl Starr.* Gretna, La.: Pelican, 1989.

Steele, Phillip W., with George Warfel. *The Many Faces of Jesse James.* Gretna, La.: Pelican, 1995.

Twain, Mark. *Life on the Mississippi.* 1874. Reprint, New York: Greystone Press, 1917.

Wilson, L. A. *Wilson's History and Directory of Southeast Missouri and Southern Illinois.* Cape Girardeau, Mo.: L. A. Wilson, 1875-76.

Yeatman, Ted P. *Frank and Jesse James: The Story Behind the Legend.* Nashville: Cumberland House, 2000.

Young, Richard Alan, and Judy Dockery. *Outlaw Tales, Legends, Myths, and Folklore from America's Middle Border.* Little Rock, Ark.: August House, 1992.

Younger, Coleman. *The Story of Cole Younger by Himself.* Chicago: Henneberry, 1903.

Zink, Wilbur A. *The Roscoe Gun Battle.* 1967. Reprint, Appleton City, Mo.: Democrat, 1989.

Newspapers

Arkadelphia (Arkansas) Ouachita Commercial, February 7, 1874.

Bolivar (Missouri) Free Press, February 5, 19, and 26, 1874; March 26, 1874; April 16, 1874.

Boonville (Missouri) Weekly Advertiser, February 6, 1874; April 14 and 28, 1882; March 19, 1897.

Boston (Massachusetts) Post, February 1874.

Chicago (Illinois) Inter-Ocean, March 20, 1874.

Chicago (Illinois) Times, March 23, 1874; May 6 and 8, 1874.

Chicago (Illinois) Tribune, February 2 and 4, 1874; March 20, 21, 22, and 23, 1874; May 8, 1874; February 2, 1875; October 13, 1895.

Clinton (Missouri) Democrat, March 20 and 21, 1874.

Dallas (Texas) Commercial, August 10, 1874.

Denison (Texas) News, August 9, 1874.

Doniphan (Missouri) Ozark Graphic, ca. 1983.

Faribault (Minnesota) Democrat, September 29, 1876.

Hamilton (Missouri) News, March 1874.

Jefferson City (Missouri) Daily Tribune, April 17, 1892.

Kansas City (Missouri) Daily Journal of Commerce, February 5, 1874; March 22, 1874.

Kansas City (Missouri) Evening Star, April 20, 1882.

Kansas City (Missouri) Times, September 27, 1872; March 14 and 16, 1874; May 22, 1874; October 25, 1874.

Lee's Summit (Missouri) Ledger, March 25, 1874.

Lexington (Missouri) Weekly Caucasian, September 5, 1874.

Liberty (Missouri) Tribune, February 6, 1874; March 20 and 27, 1874; April 7, 1874; May 22, 1874.

Little Rock Arkansas Gazette, January 18, 1874; February 3, 4, 6, 7, 24, and 26, 1874; October 2 and 9, 1966.

Little Rock (Arkansas) Republican, January 19, 20, and 30, 1874; February 2, 3, 4, 6, 13, 17, and 19, 1874.

Minneapolis (Minnesota) Tribune, September 1876.

New Orleans (Louisiana) Picayune, February 3, 1874.

New Orleans (Louisiana) Republican, February 1874.

New York (New York) Times, February 2, 3, 4, and 14, 1874.

Oklahoma City (Oklahoma) Daily Oklahoman, February 20, 1915.

Osceola (Missouri) Democrat, March 1874.

Patterson (Missouri) Times, September 10, 1874.

Pleasant Hill (Missouri) Review, November 26, 1874.

Pocahontas (Arkansas) Weekly Observer, February 10, 1874.

Poplar Bluff (Missouri) Daily American Republic, August 22, 1949.

St. Clair County (Missouri) Democrat, March 1874; August 28, 1913.

St. Joseph (Missouri) Daily Gazette, February 13, 1874.

St. Joseph (Missouri) Morning Herald, July 27, 1873.

St. Louis (Missouri) Democrat, February 4, 11, 13, and 14, 1874; April 11, 1874.

St. Louis (Missouri) Dispatch, November 22, 1873; February 5 and 10, 1874; March 16, 21, and 24, 1874; April 7 and 14, 1874; December 29, 1874.

St. Louis (Missouri) Globe, January 16, 1874; February 1, 2, 3, 4, and 6, 1874; March 20, 22, and 29, 1874; April 3, 9, and 14, 1874; August 14, 1874.

St. Louis (Missouri) Globe-Democrat, October 7-8, 1948.

St. Louis (Missouri) Post-Dispatch, October 5, 1949.

St. Louis (Missouri) Republican, March 23, 1872; February 1, 2, 3, 5, 6, 11, 13, 14, and 19, 1874; March 20, 21, 23, and 24, 1874; September 24, 1874; November 30, 1874; October 6 and 17, 1882.

St. Louis (Missouri) Times, February 1, 2, and 13, 1874; March 15, 19, 23, and 24, 1874; August 9, 1874.

Salem (Missouri) Success, February 11, 1874.

Searcy (Arkansas) Record, February 1874.

Sedalia (Missouri) Daily Bazoo, February 2 and 9, 1874.

Sedalia (Missouri) Weekly Times, February 19, 1874.

Articles, Pamphlets, and Manuscripts

Eden, M. C. "Missouri's First Train Robbery." *The Brand Book* 16, no. 2 (January 1974).

Edwards, John Newman. "A Terrible Quintette." *St. Louis Dispatch,* November 22, 1873.

McCoy, Merle J. "The Arthur McCoy Family in Missouri." *James Farm Journal* 9, no. 2 (1991).

Masnor, Lucile. "Gads Hill Train Robbery 74 Years Ago." Publication unknown (1948).

Newspaper clipping of Jim Cummins interview. Title, publication, and date unknown.

Rhodes, Henry G. "When Frank James Talked on Guns." *Fish-Fur-Game Magazine* (October 1937).

Ross, Margaret. "James Gang Again Suspected of Robbery—But This Time It's a Railroad Train." *Little Rock Arkansas Gazette,* October 9, 1966.

―――. "Stage Coach Robbery Near Hot Springs in 1874 is Attributed to the James Gang." *Little Rock Arkansas Gazette,* October 2, 1966.

Royce, Bill. "The Lacy House, and Jesse James." *Doniphan (Missouri) Ozark Graphic,* ca. 1983.

"Union Pacific Railroad . . . Nearly 150 Years of UP History and Significant Industry Events." *Info Magazine: Union Pacific Railroad* 14, no. 5 (September/October 1996).

Walker, Dale L. 1986. A Brief History of the St. Louis, Iron Mountain and Southern Railway Co. (1851-1917). Typescript.

Interviews

Harry Diesel—longtime resident of the Gads Hill area.
Tim Eaton—father once owned a store at Gads Hill.
Carl Laxton—knew Ami Dean, eyewitness to the train robbery.
Amel Martin—father was neighbor of James Sutterfield, who sold a
  horse to the outlaws.
Coker Montgomery—mother helped feed the Gads Hill outlaws.
  (Tape-recorded interview conducted by Norrid Montgomery in 1974.)
Jack Myers—grandmother was given a dime by Jesse James.
Jeanette Parker—great-granddaughter of station agent Thomas Fitz.
Bill Royce—former editor of *Ozark Graphic*, Doniphan, Missouri.
Leona Sutterfield Skelton—granddaughter of James Sutterfield.
Floyd Sutterfield—great-grandson of James Sutterfield's brother,
  Allen.
Richard Thaler—relative of conductor Chauncey Alford.
J. J. Tinsley—old-time railroad engineer.
Dale L. Walker—archivist, Missouri Pacific and Iron Mountain railroads.
Alice Fitz White—granddaughter of station agent Thomas Fitz.
Tom Williams—old-time railroad conductor.

Letters to Author

Velma Adams, 2001.
Gilbert K. Alford, Jr., 1989, 1993, 2001.
Marley Brant, 2000.
Carl W. Breihan, 1990.
Virgil Clubb, 1997.
Fern George, 2001.
Kent Dean Nichols, 2000.
Steve Nielsen, 1999.
Cheryl Oberhaus, 1997, 2000.
Jeanette Parker, 1998.
Milton F. Perry, 1989 (three letters), 1990.
Leona Sutterfield Skelton, 2001.
Phillip W. Steele, 1995, 1997.
Floyd Sutterfield, 2000.
Dale L. Walker, 1991.
Cameron Ward, 2000.

Public Records and Documents

City directories of St. Louis, 1870, 1871, and 1874.

Coroner's inquest, March 18, 1874, investigating the deaths of John Younger and Edwin B. Daniels, St. Clair County, Missouri.

The Messages and Proclamations of the Governors of the State of Missouri, vol. 5.

Record of Confederate Veterans, compiled by the United Daughters of the Confederacy, Missouri Division.

U.S. Census, Illinois, 1850 and 1860.

U.S. Census, Missouri, 1870 and 1880.

Miscellaneous

Clipping collections at the St. Louis Public Library; the State Historical Society of Missouri, Columbia; and the Missouri Historical Society, St. Louis.

1874 Iron Mountain Railway Annual Report.

Pinkerton, William A. "Train Robberies, Train Robbers, and the 'Holdup' Men." Speech presented at the annual convention of the International Association of Chiefs of Police, Jamestown, Va., 1907.

Walter B. Stevens' Scrap Book, Number 61. State Historical Society of Missouri, Columbia.

Tribune Almanac and Political Register, 1874.

Index

199